W9-DHL-057

The Mystic in Love

The Mystic In Love

A TREASURY OF WORLD MYSTICAL POETRY *edited by* SHELLEY GROSS

New York: THE CITADEL PRESS

PUBLISHED BY THE CITADEL PRESS
222 PARK AVENUE SOUTH, NEW YORK 10003
PUBLISHED SIMULTANEOUSLY IN CANADA
BY GEORGE J. McLEOD LIMITED
73 BATHURST STREET, TORONTO 2B, ONTARIO
MANUFACTURED IN THE UNITED STATES OF AMERICA
LIBRARY OF CONGRESS CATALOG CARD NUMBER: 66-24225

Dedicated With Gratitude

TO SWAMI PRABHAVANANDA,
MY BELOVED TEACHER,
AND TO MY MOTHER,
A GENTLE AND COURAGEOUS SOUL

PREFACE

The poems of a powerful religious figure of the nineteenth century directly inspired the compilation of this anthology. Swami Vivekananda, saint, scholar, mystic-poet, also struck an overwhelming response in the hearts of those who heard him at the 1893 World's Parliament of Religions in Chicago when he began his soul-piercing speech with: "Brothers and sisters of America." Upon reading his poems, letters, and lectures, one realizes that he really regarded the Western people as his own kin.

The inspiration gradually grew into an attempt to present another and, it is hoped, clearer picture of universal spiritual harmony as it emerges solely through the *poetry* of the mystics of both Eastern and Western religions. The collection is, of course, far from being a definitive one of its kind. It is to be desired that this compilation will inspire the production of a more extensive collection of mystical poetry, which will represent in greater depth the spiritual experiences of the mystics of all religions.

Far beyond any verbal expression is the editor's indebtedness to Vedanta Press (Hollywood, California) for making their bookstore and private reference library facilities available at all times for research and study. Special appreciation goes to two Vedanta Press editors for their continual enthusiasm, encouragement, and advice, without which this project would not have received its wings. Indebtedness is also extended to Benjamin Saltman, a helpful consultant during the anthology's initial stages, and to other members of the Vedanta Society of Southern California, and to my mother for proofreading assistance.

S. G.

January, 1966

ACKNOWLEDGMENTS

The author wishes to express her gratitude to the following publishers and writers for their kind permission to quote from their titles:

Asia Publishing House, India, and Radhakamal Mukerjee, *The Theory and Art of Mysticism,* R. Mukerjee; Cambridge University Press, N.Y., *Rabi'a: The Mystic,* Margaret Smith; J. M. Dent & Sons Ltd., London, *The Sisters of the Spinning Wheel and Other Sikh Poems,* Puran Singh; Ganesh & Co. Private Ltd., India, *A Seminar on Saints;* Gita Publishing House, India, *Saint Mira,* T. L. Vaswani; Islamic Research Assn., India, *'Iraqi: Song of Lovers,* A. J. Arberry; Jewish Publication Society of America, *Selected Religious Poems of Solomon Ibn-Gabirol;* Krishnamurti Writings, Inc., Calif., *The Immortal Friend,* Jiddi Krishnamurti; Luzac & Co. Ltd., London, *The Sufi Path of Love,* Margaret Smith, and *Immortal Rose,* A. J. Arberry; John Murray Ltd., London, *The Persian Mystics, Ansari and Jami;* G. A. Natesan & Co., India, *North Indian Saints,* and *Chaitanya to Vivekananda;* Pail Text Society, London, *Psalms of the Sisters;* The Ramakrishna Vedanta Centre, London, *Women Saints of East and West,* Foreword by Mrs. Vijaya Lakshmi Pandit, Introduction by Kenneth Walker, Edited by Swami Ghanananda and Sir John Stewart-Wallace, 1955; Ramakrishna Vivekananda Center, N.Y., *The Gospel of Sri Ramakrishna,* translated into English with an Introduction by Swami Nikhilananda, 1952; Shocken Books, N.Y., and James Clarke Ltd., London, *The Mystics of the Church,* Evelyn Underhill; Frederick Ungar, N.Y., *Hindu Mysticism,* S. N. Dasgupta; Duncan McFarlan, Esq., *The Flowing Light of the Godhead,* Lucy Menzies; Dr. Gopal Singh, *Sri Guru Granth Sahib;* and Frank M. Warnke, *European Metaphysical Poetry.*

Appreciation is also extended to the following publishers for granting permission to quote from their books:

Advaita Ashrama, India, *Poems by Swami Vivekananda;* Allen & Unwin Ltd., London, *Rumi: Poet and Mystic,* R. A. Nicholson, and *Classical Persian Literature,* A. J. Arberry; J. M. Dent & Sons Ltd., London, *Jacopone Da Todi: A Spiritual Biography,* Evelyn Underhill, and *The Life and Lyrics of Richard Rolle,* Frances M. M. Comper; E. P.

Dutton & Co., Inc., N.Y., "Thou Art the Path" from *The Face of Silence* by Dhan Gopal Mukerji, © 1926, "Lift My Heart," "When Wilt Thou Come?" "My Song Is in Sighing" from *The Life and Lyrics of Richard Rolle* by Frances M. M. Comper, and excerpts from the book *Jacopone Da Todi: Poet and Mystic* by Evelyn Underhill; Hillary House, N.Y., *Classical Persian Literature* (U.S.A. rights only), A. J. Arberry; The Macmillan Co., N.Y., *Songs of Kabir,* translated by Rabindranath Tagore, copyright 1915, The Macmillan Co., renewed 1942, Rathindranath Tagore; Macmillan & Co., Ltd., London, *One Hundred Poems of Kabir,* translated by Rabindranath Tagore; New American Library, N.Y., and R. B. Blakney, for *The Way of Life,* by Lao-Tzu, translated by Raymond B. Blakney, © 1955 by R. B. Blakney (published by arrangement with the New American Library, N. Y.); Sheed & Ward, Inc., London and N.Y., *Complete Works of St. Teresa,* Vol. III, translated by E. Allison Peers; Holy Trinity Church, London, *Studies of the Spanish Mystics,* E. Allison Peers; and Harvill Press, London, *Poems of St. John of the Cross,* translated by Roy Campbell.

S. G.

Contents

2. *THE SOUL AFLAME*

INTRODUCTION

Truth, goodness, love, beauty are commonly regarded as poetic ideas, but they are, in essence, spiritual facts. Man's deepest longings are spiritual, and mystic experience fulfills man's highest aspirations. Mysticism awakens the pervading, persuasive urge in man to realize himself in his totality, as a being essentially spiritual and eternal. True mysticism is neither esoteric nor strange nor fanciful. It is at once sublime, universal, and profoundly practical.

We may reasonably say that potentially all of us are mystics; the divine spirit dwells in every one of us. But for this truth to be of actual value, it must be experienced and manifested in our lives. This the mystic does. The mystic, as the truly spiritual man, is the most giving of all men. His universal vision naturally compels him to see the presence of God in all beings, and he unceasingly speaks to the essential nature of all individuals. His very existence inspires others to manifest their own higher nature. Meister Eckhart says, "What a man takes in through contemplation, that he must pour out in love." This spontaneous giving of self is an inevitable outcome of the mystic's meditation, and the state of selflessness thus attained permeates his character entirely. The great world movers have been mystics, men of God. Even today, the power of spirituality projected by a Buddha, Christ, or Ramakrishna, a Vivekananda, St. Francis, or Gandhi lives in the hearts of men and women devotees everywhere.

It may seem presumptuous to begin with an outright summation of mysticism without first entering into a step by step analysis of what it is and is not, but such an academic approach may be even more presumptuous and not within the intent of this anthology. The idea is to present the poetic expressions of the mystics themselves and let their experiences inspire the reader to reach his own conclusions as they develop from his own inner understanding. Only direct experience can open one to a spiritual intuition of what actually constitutes mysticism, beyond mere intellectual understanding. One grasps truths (leading to the Truth) to the extent that one experiences them within his own consciousness. Any analytical discussion of mysticism is limited to the realm of scholarship. As has often been said, the ultimate experience which all mystics strive for is ineffable—far transcending the highest intellectual comprehension. The mystics experience God as infinite, all-pervading, and pure Consciousness. And as the various scriptures tell us, the supreme Truth can never be expressed. Even the sacred scriptures cannot express the Absolute. Their logical conclusion is that to say what God is limits Him who is limitless. *Silence is His name*. The final validity of the mystical act must rest on the direct experience of the mystic himself. In the depths of meditation, the mystic communes with his divine Self. The effect of this union may be seen by others in the transformation of personality, in the complete purity of character.

Since mysticism alludes to an immanent as well as transcendent *dynamic state of being*, it is in itself indefinable. In the last analysis, the superconscious experience is so intensely subjective, so completely intimate, so overwhelming and final that man's lesser faculties are totally absorbed in God and merged in the boundless sea of silence.

For the sake of clarity, some preliminary notes may be helpful, and an attempt can be made to define the indefinable. The term will be interpreted as it is understood here, and in relation to its influence upon the selection of poetry. The terms "religious" and "spiritual" are used interchangeably, in the light of Vivekananda's definition of religion as "the unfoldment of the divinity already in man."

One striking element in mysticism is the *naturalness* of mystical aspiration. The mystic urge, the search for knowledge of one's true being, is inherent in man. It is the natural yearning for the most complete human fulfillment. When man becomes aware of this inner drive and desires to cultivate the awareness, the first stage of spiritual awakening may be said to have been reached. From an aesthetic-philosophic viewpoint, it may be considered in this way: What is the one supreme creative act of which man is capable?—To unite with his Creator!—to realize his oneness with the Great Cause of all causes and, simultaneously, with all of creation. This is the apex of all human endeavors. This is the mystic's supreme ideal.

With the goal of unity firmly in sight, the ascent begins. The search becomes a struggle, calling into play all the forces and energies at man's command—forces from within and from without himself. When the flash of truth shines through one's entire being, the state of illumination achieved becomes forever indisputable. The aspiring mystic seeks to reach the ocean of existence from which all life and creativity are channeled—to *know* that he "lives, moves, and has his being" in the timeless center of the universe. But most mystics will attest to the fact that spiritual unfoldment is usually preceded by years of inner preparation and earnest struggling which accompany the traveler of the religious path. The intense practicality of mysticism may be seen in the mystic's enduring efforts to concentrate all the forces of mind and heart on the Eternal Now. The illusion of a past and a future ceases to exist for the mystic as he becomes absorbed in the immediate presence of God. Every moment is an eternity to him when he lives in the bliss of God-consciousness.

The poems in this anthology will expose many diverse attitudes toward God, according to the temperament, religious orientation, and social climate influencing the particular mystic. Although an integration of faculties, a harmony between mind and heart, is always evident, one mood or another will usually predominate. The Sufi mystics are passionate; St. John of the Cross is psychological and lyrical in poetic expression; Mira Bai is God-intoxicated; St. Teresa is enraptured or anguished; Lao Tzu is rational and meditative; Kabir is full of simple joy and wisdom. Upon reading the poems, one is struck by the simplicity and immediacy of the mystics' revelations. They strike at the root of love, for they were uttered straight from the heart's illuminating awareness of divine love.

The goal is One, but the paths are many. For the mystic with a predominantly devotional temperament, the most satisfying path is through love. Love is the link between all the religious expressions of the world's mystics down through the ages. The lovers of God form a religion of their own, eternal in its intrinsic nature. The mystic is the one true lover—of God and of life, in its essence. Through him, the divergent and convergent streams of life harmoniously blend and flow without ceasing and he, in fact, becomes a living fountain of pure love, a perpetual source of joy. The mystical lover of God in His personal aspect is one who has turned away from the binding attachments to the objects of the world and has directed his entire being toward experiencing his identity with God as Love. All the passions and the diffuse energies of mind, imagination, and intellect are concentrated upon the heart of the mystic, where the Beloved dwells. He becomes wholly absorbed in the Cosmic Heart and experiences an all-embracing love radiating from the depths of his own heart. Ansārī declares:

Life in my body pulsates only for Thee

And Kabir discloses his revelation:

Whether I rise or sit down, I can
never forget Him; for the rhythm
of His music beats in my ears.

And in the *Srimad Bhagavatam* (*The Wisdom of God*)* we read:

The God of Love exists in the hearts of all. He is our very Self, and therefore very dear to us. He is Truth. He is infinity. He is

* *The Wisdom of God*, trans. by Swami Prabhavananda (Hollywood: Vedanta Press, 1943), pp. 26-27.

the omnipotent Lord. Hence should a man, freed from all selfish desires, his mind fixed on God, worship him alone.

To love God in complete surrender and whole-souled devotion is to *know* Him, to attune one's mind, heart, body, and soul to His will. Knowledge of God is perpetual awareness of His presence as manifested through all forms and names and above and beyond all activities. In the highest state of realization, perfect love and perfect wisdom merge as one, as the Truth. The man of wisdom and the lover of God are identical. When one loves God for Himself alone, one knows everything; for He is the source whence all things emerge. It has been beautifully pointed out by a Hindu monk that God-realization is the totality of knowledge. The lover of God, although a man of perfect wisdom, is actually more than a "mystic in love"—he *is* love. God is the great mystery. When one surrenders the limited individual will to God's will, one is inevitably heir to the highest wisdom.

One aim of this anthology is, then, to show the various manifestations of spiritual love and the inseparability of pure love and perfect wisdom.

Another aim is to unmask the inherent powers of poetry and expose it as the medium which is most fit to convey the varied love experiences of the mystic poets. Poetry is the highest literary expression of man's comprehensive awareness of life. Mysticism is the highest human expression (in the deepest sense of the word human) of man's comprehensive awareness of eternity.

While the focus is primarily on the mystical revelations which dominate the poems, the poetic attributes have been considered on the basis of quality, with a view toward revealing that the resources of poetry best convey progressive levels of mystical illumination. Through the medium of artistic language, employing imagery, symbology, and metaphor, the mystic's superconscious, supersensuous experience can at least be partly conveyed. Rarely will one find poetic excellence and sublime mystical expression combined in a single poem. The poems of St. John of the Cross are a notable exception, as are some of the poems of the Sufi mystics, such as 'Iraqi and Rumi, as well as those of Vivekananda. St. John of the Cross shows the ineffability of mystic experiences:

This summit all so steeply towers
And is of excellence so high
No human faculties or powers
Can ever to the top come nigh.
Whoever with its steep could vie,
Though knowing nothing would transcend
All thought, forever, without end.

In this collection, mystical expression has preponderance over poetic expression. A form of a poem, regardless of its technical precision, is dead matter until it is infused with the life of spirit and made manifest through the dynamics of language. Through the art of poetry we can come as close to understanding the mystic as a lover of God as is possible. The mystic infuses the poetic form with his deep, transcendent power of feeling, of *being*.

The poems have not been classified according to the religious traditions which inspired them, for such analysis would repudiate the book's purpose. The goal has been to demonstrate the unbreakable unity among the world's great religions and to sustain a natural flowing harmony among them. The division of chapters is purely arbitrary; two or more types of divine love may often be exhibited in a single poem. Which mood predominates will, after all, be determined by the reader's own insight. The division is for the purpose of lucidity and organization. Often, one will be struck by the harmonious blending of diverse attitudes, such as love, selflessness, strength, discrimination, and contemplation, especially evident in the poems of Vivekananda, Kabir, St. John of the Cross, and da Todi. In *A Song I Sing to Thee,* the total force of expression and the synthesis of love, devotion, wisdom, and absorption make the poem a candidate for almost any one of the chapters. But it has been included in the first chapter, for the poet primarily assumes the attitude of a servant. *To a Friend* reveals the myriad expressions of love, but it is mainly an excellent example of spiritual discrimination.

Consonant with the anthology's intent, poems were sought from all religions. Among the Jewish mystics there is much mystical poetry (especially by the Cabbalists), prayers, and hymns, but they are, unfortunately, either untranslatable in a European language or unavailable in English translation.

After some thought, it was decided to omit the seventeenth-century English poets, such as John Donne, Richard Crashaw, Henry Vaughn, and Thomas Traherne. Their works have been widely discussed and are easily available. For the same reason, mystical poems by Walt Whitman, William Wordsworth, and Robert Browning have been eliminated. The foremost concern has been to unearth poems less accessible to the general reader. Longer poems or several poems by one poet are included. This allows for greater depth of study of the writers. Material has been sought—primarily and almost exclusively—from the saints, seers, and mystics themselves; those whose very lives exhibit the undeniable success of their unceasing efforts to transcend the limitations of the ego, experience their oneness with infinity, and realize God in His fullness as Love. A melodious harmony among the poems should be transparent as the pure lovers, the mystics, sing to us with one voice.

Love

INCITED BY SOMETHING EXTERNAL
IS LIKE A SMALL LAMP
WHOSE FLAME IS FED WITH OIL,
OR LIKE A STREAM FED BY RAINS,
WHERE FLOWS STOP WHEN THE RAINS CEASE.
BUT LOVE WHOSE OBJECT IS GOD IS LIKE
A FOUNTAIN GUSHING FORTH FROM THE EARTH.
ITS FLOW NEVER CEASES,
FOR HE HIMSELF IS THE SOURCE OF THIS LOVE
AND ALSO ITS FOOD,
WHICH NEVER GROWS SCARCE.

St. Isaac

The Mystic in Love

1. Wings of Humility

THE LOVE OF DEVOTION, OBEDIENCE, AND SERVICE

ANSARI

The Path of Devotion

In this path the eye must cease to see,
And the ear to hear.
Save unto Him, and about Him.
Be as dust on His path.
Even the kings of this earth
Make the dust of His feet
The balm of their eyes.

O Lord, Give Me Eyes

O Lord, give me eyes
Which see nothing by Thy glory.
Give me a mind
That finds delight in Thy service.
Give me a soul
Drunk in the wine of Thy wisdom.

Devotion for Thee

Life in my body pulsates only for Thee,
My heart beats in resignation to Thy will.
If on my dust a tuft of grass were to grow
Every blade would tremble with my devotion for Thee!

'IRAQI

Thy Servant Let Me Be!

Enough, ye bootless cavillers,
 a truce to your complaints:
this beauty that my passion stirs
 hath moved the hearts of saints.

Such lips, such loveliness, such grace
tongue cannot tell, nor thought embrace.

The mind made captive by that tress
 is ever held in chain;
yet theirs is endless happiness
 who once His notice gain.
and I am grateful, who have known
that He is mindful of His own.

O breeze, thy servant let me be!
 if thou dost pass His way,
their tidings whisper secretly
 who in this desert stray:
tell Him the passion that I bear,
 and that I perish of despair.

The Hand of God

Not this nor that concerneth me,
In both the hand of God I see;
My heart's distraught, my brain is blind,
I have not strength of faith or mind.

The bitter taunts I hear from Thee
are sweeter far than life to me:
whom other shall I choose above
if ever I refuse Thy love?

Be merciful to me, I pray,
if thou art purposing to slay,
nor let Thy silver-gleaming arm,
that held me once, now work me harm.

No other idol I adore
but love, my play and wont of yore.
Since I am slain by Thy distress,
reproach not this my helplessness.

JAMI

One Heart, One Love

O votary of earthly idols' fane,
Why let these veils of flesh enwrap thy brain?
'Tis folly to pursue a host of loves;
A single heart can but one love contain!

O thou whose heart is torn by lust for all,
Yet vainly strives to burst these bonds of all,
This "all" begets distraction of the heart:
Give up thy heart to ONE and break with all.

God's Servant

From him who is chosen, whom God above
Deems worthy to rest in the shade of His love,

All earthly means in this world are withdrawn:
No mortal may Hold His elected in pawn.
God draws him away to Himself alone,
And to none but Him may his love be shown.
To the will of another he may not bend,
But on God alone may his hope depend.
No prayer to others must he prefer,
But be God's own servant and prisoner.

World of Love

No heart is that which love ne'er wounded: they
Who know not lovers' pangs are soulless clay.
Turn from the world, O turn thy wandering feet;
Come to the world of Love and find it sweet.

SISTER MARCELA DE CARPIO DE SAN FELIX

Amor Mysticus

My passion to prove.

Let them say to my lover
That here I lie!
The thing of His pleasure—
His slave am I.

Say that I seek Him
Only for love,
And welcome are tortures

Love giving gifts
Is suspicious and cold;
I have all, my Beloved
When thee I hold.

Hope and devotion
The good may gain;
I am but worthy
Of passion and pain.

So noble a Lord
None serves in vain,
For the pay of my love
Is my love's sweet pain.

I love Thee, to love Thee—
No more I desire;
By faith is nourished
My love's strong fire.

I kiss Thy hands
When I feel their blows;
In the place of caresses
Thou givest me woes.

But in Thy chastising
Is joy and peace.
O Master and Love
Let Thy blows not cease.

Thy beauty, Beloved,
With scorn is rife,
But I know that Thou lovest me
Better than life.

And because Thou lovest me,
Lover of mine,
Death can but make me
Utterly Thine.

I die with longing
Thy face to see;
Oh! sweet is the anguish
Of death to me!

MIRA BAI

My Refuge Art Thou

Come, O Compassionate One!
Come and meet me, Master!
Mira is Thy maid-servant:
Through the ages
Hath Mira been Thine, Thine own!
Mira falls at Thy feet:
O bless me, Beloved!

Mira hath Thou accepted
As more than Thy maid.
Mira is Thy bride, Beloved!
Protect me then,
Guard Thou Mira's honor, Lord!
At Thy Lotus-feet
Do I shelter seek!
My refuge art Thou, Beloved!

And in this broad, boundless sea
Of life art Thou my Boat.
How can I cross
Without Thee, Beloved?

When Wilt Thou Come?

I long to meet Thee, Beloved!
When wilt Thou meet
Thy humble maid, Mira?
As the dawn in beauty breaks,
I move out, every day, to seek Thee!
Ages have I spent
In quest of Thee, Beloved!
Mine eyes do ache
For a single sight of Thee!
When, O when wilt Thou come,
Beloved?

NANAK

There Is Only Thou, O God

Thou art my parent, I am Thy child,
All happiness is from Thy mercy.
No one knows Thy ends.
Highest Lord among the highest,
All that is from Thee obeys Thy will,
Thy movements, Thy pleasure,
Thou alone knowest.
Nanak, Thy slave, is a free-will offering unto Thee.

Emperors pass away, but God ever flourisheth.
There is only Thou,
There is only Thou, O God.
Neither the just nor the generous
Nor the seven regions beneath the earth shall remain.
There is One; is there any other?
There is only Thou, There is only Thou, O God.

Not the regions of the sun and the moon
Nor the seven continents, nor the seven seas,
Nor corn nor wind shall abide,
There is only Thou, There is only Thou, O God.
Our maintenance is in nobody's power but God's.
To all of us but one hope abideth;
There is One: is there any other?
There is only Thou, There is only Thou, O God.
Birds have no money in their possession.
They only depend on trees and water,
God is their Giver, There is only Thou!
There is only Thou, There is only Thou, O God!

NI'MAT-ALLAH

The Sea Is Our Essence

We are of the sea, and the sea is our essence;
why then is there this duality between us?
The world is an imaginary line before the sight;
read well that line, for it was inscribed by us.
Whatsoever we possess in both the worlds
in reality, my friend, belongs to God.

His love I keep secretly in my heart;
the less of the pain of His love is our cure.
Companions are we of the cup, comrades of the saki,
lest thou suppose that he is apart from us:
it is the assembly of love, and we are drunk—
who ever enjoyed so royal a party?
So long as Ni'mat Allah is the slave of the Lord,
the king of the world is as a beggar at his door.

RICHARD ROLLE

My Song Is in Sighing

My song is in sighing,
my life is in longing,
till I see my king
so fair in thy shining.

So fair in thy fair head,
until thy light me lead,
and in thy love me feed:
in love make me to speed
that thou be ever my meed.*

When wilt thou come,
Jesus my joy,
and cover† me of care,
and give me thee,
that I may see
thee living, evermore?

SANKARA DEVI

Prostrate at Thy Feet

Oh, my Lord, prostrate at Thy feet, I lay myself down and beseech Thee with a contrite heart to save my soul.

My soul is on the point of perishing through the poison of the venomous serpent of worldly things.

* Reward.
† Recover (from care).

On this earth all is transitory and uncertain: wealth, kinsmen, life, youth, and even the world itself.

Children, family, all are uncertain. On what shall I place reliance?

Like a drop of water on the lotus leaf, the mind is unsteady. There is no firmness in it.

There is nothing uncertain in Thy grace and no cause for fear under the shadow of Thy feet.

I, Sankara, pray to thee, O Hrishikesh, the dweller in my heart, to pilot me across this world of trouble.

Turn my heart to Thee and lead me to Thyself, Oh Lord of all blessing and all grace.

Vouchsafe unto me the truth, the right path, and Thy kindly guidance.

Thou art my mind, Thou art my destiny, Thou art my spiritual guide. Saith Sankara, steer me across the vale of sorrows.

ANGELUS SILESIUS

God's Lute

A heart that to God's will
Submits in patience mute
Loves to be touched by Him:
It serves God as His lute.

ST. TERESA OF AVILA

I Am Thine, and Born for Thee

I am Thine, and born for Thee:
What wilt Thou have done with me?

Sov'reign Lord upon Thy throne,
Endless Wisdom, One and Whole,
Goodness that dost feed my soul,
Good and great, One God alone:
Vile Thou seest me, yet Thine own,
As I sing my love for Thee.
What wilt Thou have done with me?

Thine I am, for Thou didst make me;
Thine, for Thou alone didst save me;
Thine—Thou couldst endure to have me;
For Thine own didst deign to take me.
Never once didst thou forsake me.
Ruined were I but for Thee:
What wilt Thou have done with me?

What, O good and loving Lord,
Wilt Thou have this creature do?
This Thy slave, a sinner too,
Waiting till she hears Thy word?
With Thy will in close accord,
Sweetest Love, I come to Thee:
What wilt Thou have done with me?

Take, O Lord, my loving heart:
See, I yield it to Thee whole,
With my body, life and soul

And my nature's every part.
Sweetest Spouse, my Life Thou art;
I have given myself to Thee:
What wilt Thou have done with me?

Let me live, or let me die;
Give me sickness, give me health;
Give me poverty or wealth;
Let me strive or peaceful lie.
Weakness give or strength supply—
I accept it all of Thee!
What wilt Thou have done with me?

Fame or shame may I be given;
Chasten me or make me glad;
Comfort me or make me sad;
Send me hell or grant me Heaven.
Sun, with veil for ever riven,
I have yielded all to Thee:
What wilt Thou have done with me?

Teach me, if Thou wilt, to pray;
If Thou wilt not, make me dry.
Give me love abundantly
Or unfruitful let me stay.
Sov'reign Master, I obey.
Peace I find not save with Thee:
What wilt Thou have done with me?

Give, I pray Thee, wisdom true,
Or remove it all from me;
Plenteous years I fain would see;
Years of drought and leanness too.
Days of light and darkness through,
Send me where Thou'd'st have me be:
What wilt Thou have done with me?

If in ease Thou'lt have me lie,
I accept it for Thy love;
If my constancy Thou'lt prove,
May I suffer till I die.
Tell me, sweetest Love, I cry,
How and when to die for Thee:
What wilt Thou have done with me?

Waste or fruitful land be mine,
Tabor's joy or Calvary's Cross.
Job be I, with pain and loss,
John, and on Thy breast recline.
Sterile stock or fruitful vine,
As Thou will'st it, may I be:
What wilt Thou have done with me?

Joseph, captive once in chains,
Rules in Egypt over all.
David, held in cruel thrall,
Soon a crown and kingdom gains.
Jonas suffers direst pains;
Then is cast up from the sea:
What wilt Thou have done with me?

Let me speak or hold my peace,
Rich or barren as Thou wilt;
Let the Law proclaim my guilt
Or the Gospel give release.
Let my joys or pains increase.
All my life I live in Thee:
What wilt Thou have done with me?

I am Thine, and born for Thee:
What wilt Thou have done with me?

SWAMI VIVEKANANDA

*A Song I Sing to Thee**

A song I sing. A song I sing to Thee!
Nor care I for men's comments, good or bad.
Censure or praise I hold of no account.
Servant am I, true servant of Thee Both,†
Low at Thy feet, with Sakti, I salute!

Thou standest, steadfast, ever at my back,
Hence when I turn me round, I see Thy face,
Thy smiling face. Therefore I sing again
And yet again. Therefore I fear no fear;
For birth and death lie prostrate at my feet.

Thy servant am I through birth after birth,
Sea of mercy, inscrutable Thy ways;
So is my destiny inscrutable;
It is unknown; nor would I wish to know.
Bhakti, Mukti, Japam, Tapas, all these;
Enjoyment, worship, and devotion too—
These things, and all things similar to these,
I have expelled at Thy supreme command.
But only one desire is left in me—
An intimacy with Thee, mutual!
   Take me, O Lord, across to Thee;
   Let no desire's dividing line prevent.
The eye looks out upon the universe,
Nor does it seek to look upon itself;
Why should it? It sees itself in others.
   Thou art my eyes, aye! Thou and Thou alone;
   For every living temple shrines Thy face.

* Slightly edited version.
† Purusha and Prakriti: Male and female principles.

Like to the playing of a little child
Is ev'ry attitude of mine toward Thee.
Even, at times, I dare be angered with Thee;
Even, at times, I'd wander far away;
Yet there, in greyest gloom of darkest night;
Yet there, with speechless mouth and tearful eyes,
Thou standest fronting me, and Thy sweet Face
Stoops down with loving look on face of mine.
Then, instantly, I turn my back to Thee,
And at Thy feet I fall on bended knees.
  I crave no pardon at Thy gentle hands,
  For Thou art never angry with Thy son.
Who else with all my foolish freaks would bear?
Thou art my Master! Thou my soul's real mate.

Many a time I see Thee—I am Thee!
Aye! I am Thee, and Thou, my Lord, art me!
Thou art within my speech. Within my throat
Thou art, as Vinapani,* learned, wise.
On the flow of Thy current and its force
Humanity is carried as Thou wilt.
The thunder of Thy Voice is borne upon the boom
Of crashing waves of over-leaping seas;
The sun and moon give utt'rance to Thy Voice;
Thy conversation, in the gentle breeze
Makes itself heard; in truth, in very truth,
True! True! And yet, the while, these gross precepts
Give not the message of the Higher Truth
Known to the knower!
        Lo! The sun, the moon,
The moving planets and the shining stars,
Spheres of abode by myriads in the skies;
The comet swift; the glimmering lightning-flash;

* Goddess of learning.

The firmament, expanded, infinite;
These all, observant watchful eyes behold.

Anger, desire, greed, Moha,* and the rest,†
Whence issue forth the waving of the play
Of this existence; the home wherein dwells
Knowledge, and non-knowledge—whose centre is
The feeling of small self, the "Aham!" "Aham!"—
Full of the dual sense of pleasure and of pain—
Teeming with birth and life, decay and death;
Whose arms are "The External" and "The Internal";
All things that are, down to the ocean's depths;
Up to sun, moon, and stars in spanless space;
The Mind, the Buddhi, Chitta, Ahamkâr,
The Deva, Yaksha, man and demon, all;
The quadruped, the bird, the worm, all insect life;
The atom and its compound; all that is
Animate and inanimate; all, all—
The Internal and the External—dwell
In that one common plane of existence!
  This outward presentation is of order gross,
  As hair on human brow; Aye! very gross.

On the spurs of the massive Mount Meru‡
The everlasting snowy ranges lie,
Extending miles and miles beyond more miles.
Piercing through clouds into the sky above
Its peaks thrust up in hundreds, glorious,
Brilliantly glistening, countless, snowy-white;
Flash upon flash of vivid lightning fleet.
  The sun, high in his northern solstice hung,

* Delusion.
† The six passions.
‡ A fabulous mountain round which the planets are said to revolve.

With force of thousand rays concentrating,
Pours down upon the mountain floods of heat,
Furious as a billion thunderbolts,
From peak to peak.
  Behold! The radiant sun
Swoons, as it were, in each. Then melts
The massive mountain with its crested peaks!
Down, down, it falls, with a horrific crash!
  Water, with water lies commingled now;
And all has passed like to a passing dream.

When all the many movements of the mind
Are, by Thy grace, made one, and unified,
The light of that unfoldment is so great
That, in its splendor, it surpasses far
The brilliance of ten thousand rising suns.
Then, sooth, the sun of Chit* reveals itself.
And melt away the sun and moon and stars,
High heaven above, the nether worlds, and all!
This universe seems but a tiny pool
Held in a hollow caused by some cow's hoof.
  —This is the reaching of the region which
Beyond the plane of the External lies.

  Calmed are the clamors of the urgent flesh;
The tumult of the boastful mind is hushed;
Cords of the heart are loosened and set free;
Unfastened are the bondages that bind;
Attachment and delusion are no more!
  Aye! There sounds sonorous the Sound
Void of vibration. Verily! Thy Voice!
  Hearing that Voice, Thy servant, reverently,
Stands ever ready to fulfil Thy work.

* Knowledge.

2. *The Soul Aflame*

THE LOVE OF PASSION, BEAUTY, AND YEARNING

ANONYMOUS
(14th Century)

*Quia Amore Langueo**

In a valley of this restless mind
I sought in mountain and in mead,
Trusting a true love for to find.
Upon a hill then took I heed;
A voice I heard, and near I yede,†
In great dolor complaining tho:
See, dear soul, how my sides bleed:
Quia amore langueo.

. . .

I am true love that false was never;
My sister, man's soul, I loved her thus.
Because we would in no wise dissever
I left my Kingdom glorious.
I purveyed her a palace full precious;
She fled, I followed, I loved her so
That I suffered this pain piteous,
Quia amore langueo.

* "For I Am Faint With Love."
† Go.

ANSARI

O Lord, Intoxicate Me

O Lord, intoxicate me with the wine
Of Thy love.
Place the chains of Thy slavery on
My feet;
Make me empty of all but Thy love,
And in it destroy me and bring me
Back to life.
The hunger Thou hast awakened culminates
In fulfillment.

This Heart Afire

Do not, O God, put out
This flickering lamp!
Cast not this heart afire with Thee for Thee
Into the furnace of desire!

Oh! God! Rend not
My patched-up sail
Nor drive my broken bark
From the river of knowledge.

The Flame of Thy Love Glows

O Lord, to find Thee is my desire
But to comprehend Thee
Is beyond my strength.
Remembering Thee is solace
To my sorrowing heart.

Thoughts of Thee are my Constant Companions.
I call upon Thee night and day.
The flame of Thy love glows
In the darkness of my night.

'ATTAR

I Call on Thee

When in the night of dryness
I call on Thee,
The vessel of my spirit
Goes riding free.

And where the mighty ocean
Before me lies
A hundred salty torrents
Flood from mine eyes.

I make for me a vessel
Out of Thy name,
And into distant waters
I sail the same.

And by that mighty motion
Upon each breath
My spirit everlasting
Far ventureth.

Love's Coming

When unto me Love came
He set my heart aflame;
My heart exultant there
Bragged of its sweetheart fair.

In quietude complete
I sat in my retreat
Until Love passionate
Hammered upon my gate.

The tree of all my mirth
Love rooted out of earth;
Whatever I did own
Was in tumult thrown.

They said: "His sweet delight
Is silver-bosomed, bright";
Till in desire, behold
My face was sick as gold.

The peacock of His face
Made a display of grace;
My reason, like a fly,
Stood waving hands on high.

My heart His face beheld
And like an ocean welled,
And was there ever sea,
Whose waves all jewels be?

Since Attar in desire
Hath a heart all afire
Each single breath he takes
In glowing ember breaks.

BABA TAHIR

Burning for Thee

A nameless, homeless braggart,
  A Kalendar am I:
By day the world's my parish,
  At night with weary sigh
  On bed of stones I lie.

No moth e'er knew such burning,
  No madman bore such dree:
Ants have their nests for shelter,
  For serpents holes there be;
  But roof is none for me.

The stony earth for pillow,
  For coverlet the air;
My only sin was loving—
  Do all Thy lovers share
  This torment that I bear?

DHU'L-NUN

Thy Love, My Only Goal

I die, and yet not dies in me
The ardor of my love for Thee,
Nor hath Thy love, my only goal,
Assuaged the fever of my soul.

To Thee alone my spirit cries;
In Thee my whole ambition lies,
And still Thy Wealth is far above
The poverty of my small love.

I turn to Thee in my request,
And seek in Thee my final rest;
To Thee my loud lament is brought;
Thou dwellest in my secret thought.

However long my sickness be,
This wearisome infirmity,
Never to men will I declare
The burden Thou hast made me bear.

To Thee alone is manifest
The heavy labor of my breast,
Else never kin or neighbors know
The brimming measure of my woe.

A fever burns below my heart
And ravages my every part;
It hath destroyed my strength and stay,
And smoldered all my soul away.

Guidest Thou not upon the road
The rider wearied by his load,
Delivery from the steeps of death
The traveller as he wandereth?

Didst Thou not light a Beacon too
For them that found the Guidance true
But carried not within their hand
The faintest glimmer of its brand?

O then to me Thy Favour give
That, so attended, I may live;
And overwhelm with ease from Thee
The rigor of my poverty.

FAKHIR AL-DIN MAS'UDI

Deep in the Desert

Deep in the desert of Thy love uncrossed
Wander like me a thousand wretches lost.
Love to their anguish myriad guises lends,
Thy beauty is the medicine of their care,
Union with Thee, their hope that kills despair.
Unless with loving hand Thou lead them on,
Their souls will go the way their hearts have gone.
Where Thou art throned above our human fate,
Fraud and religion bear an equal rate;
Milk of Thy grace the wise old man, world-soiled,
Tastes and becomes again a new-born child.

'IRAQI

Thy Lover Cannot Eat

Thy lover cannot eat nor sleep,
his couch is drenched with tears;
though beauty strikes his spirit deep,
of death he has no fears.

Love's lesson he has learnt by heart,
still fasting and at prayer;
and to the lover's wilful dart
his bosom he doth bare.

No more may he his right defend,
no strength has he to shield;
but on the pathway of the Friend
his heart and spirit yield.

With true resolve and purpose high,
like him who pens this song,
through storm he battles to the sky
love's fearful path along.

Show Now Thy Face

How long shall I the truth conceal?
I love Thee! Let the echoes peal!
Since Thou hast shown Thy face to me,
I yield my soul right willingly.

Thou lovers well may pardoned be,
since never was a love like Thee:
and shall the eye be satisfied
that hath Thy beauty once descried?

Show now Thy face, and do not turn
from him whose heart with woe doth burn.
Now send me Thou repose or strife:
Thou art the ruler of my life.

O ye who chide with counsel drear,
such counsel love doth never hear.
Though I am banished from Thy face,
Thine image ever I embrace.

So dwellest Thou within my heart,
I think that in my sight Thou art:
but ah, my soul! Dream not so vain:
thou canst not to such dreams attain.

My Mad Heart Takes the Cup of Love

Again my mad heart takes the cup
of love, upon love's breast reclining:
again my soul is yielded up,
to love's enfolding might resigning.

The wine hath filled my weary brain
with vapors from love's censer blowing:
give wine, for sorrow once again
its melancholy head is showing.

The loveliness of Thy fair face
my mind doth haunt, my heart is stealing;
else love had never found a place
within the heart, such joy revealing.

Love's pigeon to my heart doth fly
a message from my Lover giving,
and gladly for His sake I die,
with Him forever to be living.

My Yearning Heart

My yearning heart is nigh to Thee,
my frame in prison far:
why hidest Thou Thy face from me?
Love should not know a bar.

Thou art the leech, and I am sick,
Thou weary, I am fain;
Thy charming glance, like arrow quick,
hath pierced my heart again.

Though wine hath never touched my lip,
with yearning I am drunk:
upon Thy sea of pain my ship
of life and hope is sunk.

O Thou Who mak'st to shine above
yon newly-risen sun,
within the desert of Thy love
my heart is spent and done.

I Still Beseech Thee

Thy love hath oped my spirit's eye,
to Thee my yearning heart doth cry;
my night of grief turns not to day
because Thy face is turned away.

Thou thinkest not on us, who pour
our heart's petitions at Thy door.
Shall ever thus my spirit's peace
this yearning break, that will not cease?

My soul, a bird, hath flown from nest
and only in Thy street will rest:
keep me no more in banishment,
lest of our love the veil be rent.

At last, O spirit-gladdening sun,
let fall Thy shade on me fordone:
be honour or contempt my lot,
I still beseech Thee, pass me not.

Each moment that apart from Thee
I live in thought and memory
a weary history doth make
of heart's desire and spirit's ache.

Of Man's Perfection in Love

O minstrel, raise thy plaintive melody,
and let thy song be tender to my soul:
upon the subtle ninefold modes of love
display the secrets of a lover's heart.
One moment parted from the Friend, I die:
revive my heart with thy life-giving stream
that I may come into the lovers' ring
and grace the lovers' circle. Let me pass
one moment from the world, and for an hour
I will not heed my selfhood: being lost
to this false being, let me swiftly move
to realms of drunkenness where, like the drunk,
I will commence the dance, and raise the cry
of yearning love—for truly I do yearn

for my Beloved—standing in the field
of high ambition. I will shake my wings
like sacrificial bird, and fly at last
from empty word to true reality.
Then will I tell in order, each by each,
the beauty of the Friend, the lover's love.

ST. JOHN OF THE CROSS

Without God I Cannot Live

I live without inhabiting
Myself—in such a wise that I
Am dying that I do not die.

Within myself I do not dwell
Since without God I cannot live.
Reft of myself, and God as well,
What serves this life (I cannot tell)
Except a thousand deaths to give?
Since waiting here for life I lie—
And die because I do not die.

This life I live in vital strength
Is loss of life unless I win You:
And thus to die I shall continue
Until in You I live at length.
Listen (my God!) my life is in You.
This life I do not want, for I
Am dying that I do not die.

Thus in your absence and your lack
How can I in myself abide
Nor suffer here a death more black
Than ever was by mortal died.

For pity of myself I've cried
Because in such a plight I lie
Dying because I do not die.

The fish that from the stream is lost
Derives some sort of consolation
That in his death he pays the cost
At least of death's annihilation.
To this dread life with which I'm crossed
What fell death can compare, since I,
The more I live, the more must die.

When thinking to relieve my pain
I in the sacraments behold You
It brings me greater grief again
That to myself I cannot fold You.
And that I cannot see you plain
Augments my sorrow, so that I
Am dying that I do not die.

If in the hope I should delight,
Oh Lord, of seeing You appear,
The thought that I might lose your sight,
Doubles my sorrow and my fear.
Living as I do in such fright,
And yearning as I yearn, poor I
Must die because I do not die.

Oh rescue me from such a death
My God, and give me life, not fear;
Nor keep me bound and struggling here
Within the bonds of living breath.
Look how I long to see You near,
And how in such a plight I lie
Dying because I do not die!

I shall lament my death betimes,
And mourn my life, that it must be
Kept prisoner by sins and crimes
So long before I am set free:
Ah God, my God, when shall it be?
When I may say (and tell no lie)
I live because I've ceased to die?

*Make the Last Surrender**

Oh who my grief can mend!
Come, make the last surrender that I yearn for,
And let there be an end
Of messengers you send
Who bring me other tidings than I burn for.

All those that haunt the spot
Recount your charm, and wound me worst of all,
Babbling I know not what
Strange rapture, they recall,
Which leaves me stretched and dying where I fall.

How can you thus continue
To live, my life, where your own life is not?
With all the arrows in you
And, like a target, shot
By that which in your breast he has begot.

Why then did you so pierce
My heart, nor heal it with your touch sublime?
Why, like a robber fierce,
Desert me every time
And not enjoy the plunder of your crime?

* Abridged.

Come, end my sufferings quite
Since no one else suffices for physician:
And let mine eyes have sight
Of you, who are their light,
Except for whom I scorn the gift of vision.

Reveal your presence clearly
And kill me with the beauty you discover,
For pains acquired so dearly
From Love, cannot recover
Save only through the presence of the lover.

Oh brook of crystal sheen
Could you but cause, upon your silver fine,
Suddenly to be seen
The eyes for which I pine
Which in my inmost heart my thoughts design!

MECHTHILD OF MAGDEBURG

I Call Thee

I call Thee with profound desire
And piteous voice.
I wait for Thee with a heavy heart:
I cannot rest, I burn without respite
In Thy flaming love.
I seek Thee with all my might:
Had I the power of a giant
Thou wert quickly lost
If I came upon Thy footprints.

Ah! Love! Run not so far ahead
But rest a little lovingly
That I may catch thee up!

Set Me on Fire

O soaring eagle! darling lamb!
O glowing spark! Set me on fire!
How long must I endure this thirst?
One hour is already too long,
A day is as a thousand years
When Thou art absent!
Should this continue for eight days
I would rather go down to Hell
(Where indeed I already am!)
Than that God should hide Himself
From the loving soul;
For that were anguish greater than human death,
Pain beyond all pain.
The nightingale must ever sing
Because its nature is love;
Whoso would take that from it
Would bring it death.
Ah! Mighty Lord! Look on my need!

MIRA BAI

In Quest of Thee

Beloved!
I wander still
In quest of Thee!
I am athirst
For Thy Eternal Love!

I long to make
My body a lamp—
The wick whereof will be
My tender heart.
And I would fill the lamp
With the scented oil
Of my love for Thee!
Then let it burn,
Day and night,
At thy shrine,
Beloved!

I can no longer bear
To be away from Thee.
Make me Thine own!
Make me like Thee!
And make me pure
As Thou art pure,
Beloved!

My Heart Is Athirst

Where shall I meet Thee,
O Spouse of my soul?
My heart is athirst
For a glimpse of Thy Lotus-face.
Behold! Each day I pine for Thee:
I live in Death!
I know my bed
Doth over the gallows lie:
How can I sleep?

Beloved! Thy throne is in yon sky!
Betwixt Thee and me
Lie stretched the spaces of many sins:
How, then, can I meet Thee?

The ache of wounds
Is to the wounded known!
The pain of him who suffers
Is known alone to the suffering ones!

Within me throbs the ache
Of longing and love for Thee!
And I wander far and wide!
I cry: Who will cure
My wounded heart
My anguish, alas! doth greater grow
Each day, my longing grows:
I cry for Him whom heart may heal!

The Bread of My Soul Art Thou!

The Bread of my soul art Thou!
The Strength of my heart art Thou!
The Treasure of my life art Thou!
Methinks I hear Thy Voice,
I hear the sound of Thy Flute.

Sometimes I see Thee
Coming quick from a grove,
Beautiful and bright!
And over Thee I see
A touch of Fire,
A Flame of Beauty!
And from the Flame doth come
A Voice: but I understand it not.

And I sob and cry:
"O meet me, Master!"
No more separation!

Sometimes I see,
When all is dark,
That in the Heart within
Doth shine a Light, Thy Light!
And then I cry:
"I have seen
What I have seen!"

And again I cry:
"Holy! Holy! Holy!
The Holy One have I seen!"
And a Voice I hear again:
It speaketh to my heart:
"Open to Me,
For I come quickly!"
I open! But Thou art gone!

RICHARD ROLLE

When Wilt Thou Come?

When wilt thou come to comfort me
and bring me out of care,
And give thee to me, that I may see
and have for ever more?
Thy love is ever sweetest to me
of all that ever were.
Mine heart for love when shall it burst
that languishing it may no more.
Fall all on love mine heart is set
and I am fain to go.

I stood astonied* in still morning
of one loveliest of lore.†
My love is long longing;
it draweth me to my day,
the bond of love burning,
for it holdeth me ay
from place and from playing
till that I get it may,
the sight of my sweeting
that wedeth never away.
In wealth be our waking
without noy‡ of night.
My love is lasting
and longeth to that sight.

Lift My Heart

In love Thou wound my thought,
And lift my heart to Thee.
My soul Thou dear hast bought,
Thy lover make it be.
Thee I covet,
This world nought,
And from it I flee.
Thou art That I have sought.
Thy face when may I see?

* Stunned, dazed.
† Can be used for "behavior."
‡ Annoyance, harm.

ST. TERESA OF AVILA

Yearning for Thee

Ah, my God, without Thee
Life goes sadly by,
And my yearning for Thee
Makes me long to die.

What a tedious journey
Is our exile here!
Dreary is the sojourn,
Hard indeed to bear!
Oh, beloved Master,
Rescue me, I cry,
Since my yearning for Thee
Makes me long to die.

Dark is this existence;
Bitter is its thrall:
Life that's lived without Thee
Is not Life at all.
Oh, my sweetest Lover,
Miserable am I,
And my yearning for Thee
Makes me long to die.

Come, O death, come kindly;
Loose me from my pain.
Sweet the blows thou dealest:
Liberty they gain.
Blest are they, Beloved,
That have Thee ever by.
Thus my yearning for Thee
Makes me long to die.

Earthly love that's earthly
Clings to earth, its home;
Love divine sighs ever
For the life to come.
None can live, Redeemer,
Save when Thou art nigh,
So my yearning for Thee
Makes me long to die.

This our earthly desert
Is a vale of woe.
Life has no beginning
Till to Heaven we go.
Grant me, O my Saviour,
Thither soon to fly,
Since my yearning for Thee
Makes me long to die.

Who is he that shrinks from
Death, however keen,
Since the life it brings is
Boundless and serene?
Such it is to love Thee,
Lord, eternally,
And my yearning for Thee
Makes me long to die.

My afflicted spirit
Sighs and faints away.
Who from his Beloved
Absent long can stay?
Let my bitter suffering
Vanish speedily,
Since my yearning for Thee
Makes me long to die.

Soon the fish enmeshed
By the crafty snare
Finds its torture ended:
Kindly death is there.
Like the fish I suffer
When Thou art not nigh;
And my yearning for Thee
Makes me long to die.

Vainly, Lord and Master,
Strive I after sight:
Thou, the Ever-Hidden,
Endest not my plight.
And my kindling passion
Drags from me the cry:
Oh, my yearning for Thee
Makes me long to die.

Hardly hast Thou enter'd
In my breast to stay
Than I fear, my Saviour,
Lest Thou flee away.
Then my deep affliction
Causes me to sigh:
How my yearning for Thee
Makes me long to die.

Oh, my Lord, I pray Thee,
End my agony:
Succor this Thy servant
As she sighs for Thee.
Rend apart these fetters:
Then how happy I,
Since my yearning for Thee
Makes me long to die.

Yet, Beloved Master,
Great has been my sin;
Meet it is I suffer,
Penitence to win.
May my weeping reach Thee;
Listen to my cry,
As my yearning for Thee
Makes me long to die.

TUKARAM

My Heart Cries to Thee

As on the bank the poor fish lies
And gasps and writhes in pain,
Or, as a man with anxious eyes
Seeks hidden gold in vain,
So is my heart distressed, and cries
To come to thee again.
  Thou knowest, Lord, the agony
  Of the lost infant's wail
  Yearning his mother's face to see.
  (How oft I tell this tale.)
  O, at thy feet the mystery
  Of the dark world unveil.
The fire of this harassing thought
Upon my bosom prays.
Why is it I am thus forgot?
(O, who can know thy ways?)
Nay, Lord, thou seest my hapless lot;
Have mercy, Tuka says.

SWAMI VIVEKANANDA

My Play Is Done

I

Ever rising, ever falling with the waves of time, still
rolling on I go
From fleeting scene to scene ephemeral, with life's
currents' ebb and flow.
Oh! I am sick of this unending farce; these shows
they please no more,
This ever running, never reaching, nor e'en a distant
glimpse of shore!
From life to life I'm waiting at the gates; alas, they
open not.
Dim are my eyes with vain attempt to catch one
ray long sought.
On little life's high narrow bridge I stand and see
below
The struggling, crying, laughing throng. For what?
No one can know.
In front yon gates stand frowning dark, and say:
"No farther way,
This is the limit; tempt not Fate, bear it as best
you may;
Go mix with them and drink this cup and be as
mad as they.
Who dares to know but comes to grief; stop then,
and with them stay."
Alas for me, I cannot rest. This floating bubble,
earth—
Its hollow form, its hollow name, its hollow death
and birth—

For me is nothing. How I long to get beyond the
crust
Of name and form! Ah, ope the gates; to me they
open must.
Open the gates of light, O Mother to me, Thy tired
son.
I long, oh, long to return home! Mother, my play is
done.

II

You sent me out in the dark to play, and wore a
frightful mask;
Then hope departed, terror came, and play became
a task.
Tossed to and fro, from wave to wave in this
seething, surging sea
Of passions strong and sorrows deep, grief *is,* and
joy *to be,*
Where life is living death, alas! and death—who
knows but 'tis
Another start, another round of this old wheel of
grief and bliss?
Where children dream bright, golden dreams, too
soon to find them dust,
And aye look back to hope long lost and life a mass
of rust!
Too late, the knowledge age doth gain; scarce from
the wheel we're gone.
When fresh young lives put their strength to the
wheel, which thus goes on
From day to day and year to year. 'Tis but
delusion's toy,
False hope its motor; desire, nave; its spokes are
grief and joy.

I go adrift and know not whither. Save me from
this fire!
Rescue me, merciful Mother, from floating with
desire!
Turn not to me Thy awful face, 'tis more than I
can bear,
Be merciful and kind to me, to chide my faults
forbear.
Take me, O Mother, to those shores where strifes
for ever cease;
Beyond all sorrows, beyond tears, beyond e'en
earthly bliss;
Whose glory neither sun nor moon nor stars that
twinkle bright,
Nor flash of lightning can express. They but reflect
its light.
Let never more delusive dreams veil off Thy face
from me.
My play is done; O Mother, break my chains and
make me free!

3. *Lifting the Veil*

THE LOVE OF PURIFICATION, INTRO-SPECTION, AND CONCENTRATION

JACOPONE DA TODI

Watchfulness Over the Senses

Friend, beware lest thou fall:
Beware!

First, beware thy ghostly foe,
Who in friend's disguise doth go.
Trust him not, he brings thee woe:
Beware!

Turn thine Eyes away from ill,
Evil sights may wound thy will;
Healing hurt thee deeper still:
Beware!

Evil tongues a snare will set;
Stone thine Ears: nay, closer yet!
Lest they catch thee in a net:
Beware!

Put a bridle on thy Taste:
Plenty turns to poisonous waste,
Then comes Luxury in haste:
Beware!

Scents and savors perilous,
Fragrances insidious—
God hath set them far from us:
Beware!

God is grieved by sinful Touch;
Set thy guard and keep thy watch!
Thou may'st perish in its clutch:
Beware!

From thy kindred dwell apart,
Lest they shake thy steadfast heart,
Lest they cause thee dole and smart;
Beware!

Watch! thy friends will throng around,
Run like ants, like ants abound,
Dry thy roots in God's own ground:
Beware!

O beware! lest evil thought
Wound and bring thy mind to naught;
Sicken all thy soul distraught:
Beware!

Lord, Thou Hast Shown Me

Lord, Thou hast shown me now,
In Thy fair holiness,
Mine utter nothingness;
Yea, less than nothing I!
And from this gazing springs
An eager humbleness;
Prisoned in wretchedness,

    My will but lives to die.
    My mind's humility
Is not made vile by ill,
But, loving virtue still,
    Through vileness, gains Thy height.

I cannot be re-born
  Till mine own self be dead;
  My life out-poured, out-shed,
    Sheer essence to renew:
On glorious Nothingness
    He only can be fed,
    Whom God Himself hath led;
    Here man hath naught to do.
    O glorious state and true!
In Nothingness to cease,
Desire and mind at peace
    In calmness infinite.

Ah! how my earth-bound thoughts
  Are hideous and mean,
  Beside those heights serene,
    Where virtue's treasures be.
That Deep whereon I gaze,
    I cannot swim therein,
    I must be swallowed clean,
    Like men who drown at sea.
    Shoreless Infinity!
I sink in Thee, the Whole:
Thy fulness storms my soul,
    Thou Sweetness and Thou Light!

MUHAMMAD IQBAL

Make Self Strong, and Thou Wilt Endure

Thou hast being, and art thou afraid of not-being?
O foolish one, thy understanding is at fault.
Since I am acquainted with the harmony of Life,
I will tell thee what is the secret of Life—
To sink into thyself like the pearl,
Then to emerge from thine inward solitude;
To collect sparks beneath the ashes,
And become a flame and dazzle men's eyes.

Move round thyself! Be a circling flame!
What is life but to be freed from moving round others
And to regard thyself as the Holy Temple?
Beat thy wings and escape from the attractions of Earth;
Like birds, be safe from falling.

JAMI

Thou and We Are Not Separate

O Thou whose sacred precincts none may see,
Unseen Thou makest all things seen to be;
  Thou and we are not separate, yet still
Thou hast no need of us, but we of Thee.

None by endeavor can behold Thy face,
Or access gain without prevenient grace;
  For every man some substitute is found,
Thou hast no peer, and none can take Thy place.

Of accident or substance Thou hast naught,
Without constraint of cause Thy grace is wrought;
  Thou canst replace what's lost, but if Thou'rt lost,
In vain a substitute for Thee is sought.

In me Thy beauty love and longing wrought:
Did I not see Thee how could'st Thou be sought?
  My love is as a mirror in the which
Thy beauty into evidence is brought.

O Lord, none but Thyself can fathom Thee,
Yet every mosque and church doth harbor Thee;
  I know the seekers and what 'tis they seek—
Seekers and sought are all comprised in Thee.

Make My Heart Pure

Make my heart pure, my soul from error free,
Make tears and sighs my daily lot to be,
  And lead me on Thy road away from self,
That lost to self I may approach to Thee!

Set enmity between the world and me,
Make me averse from worldly company:
  From other objects turn away my heart,
So that it is engrossed with love to Thee.

How were it, Lord, if Thou should'st set me free
From error's grasp and cause me truth to see?
  Guebres* by scores Thou makest Musulmans,
Why, then, not make a Musulman of me?

* Magians and Zoroastrians.

My lust for this world and the next efface,
Grant me the crown of poverty and grace
  To be partaker in Thy mysteries,
From paths that lead not towards Thee turn my face.

JENTI

The Pure Mind

The Seven Factors* of the awakened mind—
Seven ways whereby we may Nibbana win—
All, all have I developed and made ripe,
Even according to the Buddha's word.

For I therein have seen as with mine eyes
The Bless'd, the Exalted One. Last of all lives
Is this that makes up Me. The round of births
Is vanquished—Ne'er shall I be again!

LAO-TZU

Be Humble

The great land is a place
To which the streams descend;
It is the concourse and
The female of the world:
Quiescent, underneath,
It overcomes the male.

* Mindfulness, research in the Dhamma, energy, joy, serenity, concentration, equanimity.

By quietness and by humility
The great land then puts down the small
And gets it for its own;
But small lands, too, absorb the great
By their subservience.
Thus some lie low, designing conquest's ends;
While others lowly are, by nature bent
To conquer all the rest.

The great land's foremost need is to increase
The number of its folk;
The small land needs above all else to find
Its folk more room to work.
That both be served and each attain its goal
The great land should attempt humility.

Once Grasp the Great Form

Once grasp the great Form without form,
And you roam where you will
With no evil to fear,
Calm, peaceful, at ease.

At music and viands
The wayfarer stops.
But the Way, when declared,
Seems thin and so flavorless!

It is nothing to look at
And nothing to hear;
But used, it will prove
Inexhaustible.

FRANCIS QUARLES

Our Meditation Upon God

When thy ambitious knowledge would attempt
So high a task as God, she must exempt
All carnal sense; Thy Reason must release
Her pow'r, thy Fancy must be bound to the peace;
Thy spirits must be rapt, they must exile
Thy Flesh, and keep a Sabbath, for a while:
Thou must forget thy self, and take strong Bands
Of thy own thoughts, and shake eternal hands
With thy rebellious Lust; discard and clear
Thy heart of all Ideas; then with Fear
And holy Reverence, thou must think of One,
As though he were not to be thought upon:
Conceive a Spiritual, a most perfect Being,
Pure, Simple; At the self-same instant, seeing
Things Present, Past, and Future; One whose Might,
Whose Wisdom, Justice, Mercy (in a height
Above Exceeding) is Himself, being great
Without a Quantity, and most Complete
Without Degrees: Eternal, without space,
Of Time: At all times present, without Place:
Think thus, and when thy thoughts can soar no higher,
Stay there, stand humbly silent, and admire.

To God

Glorious, and Great; whole power did divide
  The waves and made them Walls on either side,
  That didst appear in Cloven Tongues of Fire:

Divide my thoughts; and with thy Self inspire
My soul; O Cleave my Tongue, and make it scatter
Various Expressions in a various Manner:
That like the painful Bee, I may derive
From sundry Flowers to store my slender Hive;
Yet may my thoughts, not too divided be,
But they may mix again, and fix in Thee.

JACOB REVIUS

God's Likeness

A clear pool alone reflects the sun,
Not a dirty sump, or fountain which doth run:
For in water impure or water ever roll'd
The clean reflection instantly is spoil'd.

O Soul that will God's image hold within,
Shun undue motion and reject all sin;
For the likeness of God can show itself but there
Where the heart is still, the spirit clear and fair.

On the Same

A narrow pool cannot in sense contain
Reflection more than one, or faces twain;
Of necessity one holds the other out.
Mark well, O Man, the meaning free from doubt:
Wilt thou God's picture faithfully present,
Drive from thy heart those pictures devil-sent,
Of God, of lust, or pride; the face divine
Only alone within thy heart will shine.

RUMI

The Truth Within Us

'Twas a fair orchard, full of trees and fruit
And vines and greenery. A Sufi there
Sat with eyes closed, his head upon his knee,
Sunk deep in meditation mystical.
"Why," asked another, "dost thou not behold
These Signs of God the Merciful displayed
Around thee, which He bids us contemplate?"
"The signs," he answered, "I behold within;
Without is naught but symbols of the Signs."

What is all beauty in the world? The image,
Like quivering boughs reflected in a stream,
Of that eternal Orchard which abides
Unwithered in the hearts of Perfect Men.*

The Relativity of Evil

There is no absolute evil in the world: evil is relative.
Recognize this fact.
In the realm of Time there is nothing that is not a foot to one and a fetter to another.
To one a foot, to another a fetter; to one a poison, to another sweet and wholesome as sugar.
Snake-venom is life to the snake, but death to man; the sea is a garden to sea-creatures, but to the creatures of earth a mortal wound.

* An early parallel occurs in the legend of Rabi'a. One day in spring-time she entered her house and bowed her head. "Come out," said the woman-servant, "and behold what God hath made." "Come in," Rabi'a answered, "and behold the Maker."

Zayd, though a single person, may be a devil to one and an angel to another:
If you wish him to be kind to you, then look on him with a lover's eye.
Do not look on the Beautiful with your own eye: behold the Sought with the eye of the seeker.
Nay, borrow sight from Him: look on His face with His eye.
God hath said, "Whoso belongs to Me, I belong to him: I am his eye and his hand and his heart."
Everything loathly becomes lovely when it leads you to your Beloved.

The Mystic Way

Plug thy low sensual ear, which stuffs like cotton
Thy conscience, and makes deaf thine inward ear.
Be without ear, without sense, without thought,
And hearken to the call of God, "*Return*!"

Our speech and action is the outer journey,
Our inner journey is above the sky.
The body travels on its dusty way;
The spirit walks, like Jesus, on the sea.

ANGELUS SILESIUS

Parts of God

The sea is sea throughout
Every finest spray of sea.
Say how in God pure souls
Aught else but God may be!

The Source Lies in Us

Thou needst not cry to God,
The Spring wells up in thee.
Unless thou stop its source,
It will flow eternally.

Our Double Nature

Two eyes our souls possess:
While one is turned on time,
The other seeth things
Eternal and sublime.

SUNDARI-NANDA

Concentrate

Behold, Nanda, the foul compound, diseased,
Impure! Compel thy heart to contemplate
What is not fair to view. So steel thyself
And concentrate the well-composed mind.
As with this body, so with thine; as with
Thy beauty, so with this—thus shall it be
With this malodorous, offensive shape,
Wherein the foolish only take delight.
So look thou on it day and night with mind
Unfalteringly steadfast, till alone,
By thine own wit, delivered from the thrall
Of beauty, thou dost gain vision serene.

TAYUMANAVAR

O Mind, Be Clear

O Mind, who art like the gold
in ornaments, being the texture of all things—
wilt thou not ripen of thyself and become
the fruit of Samadhi,
be clear of thy imperfections?
For I have no friend like thee,
Surely Thou art like the Divine Grace itself,
Thou art the Guru, the bond inseparable.

For many days I had bliss with Thee,
and now, because of separation from Me,
if Thou liest as one dead, inert,
truly I shall salute the very direction of Thy repose.
Through Thee I shall be freed of grief,
and inherit the bliss of Freedom.

4. *The Intellectual Fire*

THE LOVE OF CONTEMPLATION, DISCRIMINATION, AND TRUTH

'ATTAR

Fire

It is a raging sea of fire
The Darling's beauty to desire:
Be thou a lover, thou shalt blaze,
For so were ever beauty's ways.

Consider where the candle's light
Gleams suddenly in radiance bright,
How should it ever be presumed
The moth will not be all consumed?

When first the lover shyly strode
Upon love's everlasting road,
In prone humility he fell
A shadow upon earth to dwell.

And when a little space was past
No shadow more at all he cast,
For in a far and lofty place
The sun conceals his radiant face.

If thou wouldst know love's mystery,
Leave faith and infidelity;
When love is come, he banisheth
Both infidelity and faith.

A many thousand travellers,
And each his loverhood avers;
And in this ring that is the Way
Hallej the shining bezel lay.

It is a task both hard and high
This mystic Way to travel by.
And where a thousand travellers be
But one alone the Path can see.

How knowest thou who travelleth there?
For on this Road the wayfarer
When he doth take the first of steps
High o'er the seventh heaven leaps.

Who'er the pearl of Meaning true
Within this Ocean doth pursue,
Here and beyond in noble pride
He shall eternally abide.

'Attar who on this road doth fare
Hath come unto a station, where
Body and soul he dwells above
And hath transcended Hate and Love.

All-Pervading Consciousness

And as His Essence all the world pervades
Naught in Creation is, save this alone.
Upon the waters has He fixed His Throne,
This earth suspended in the starry space,
Yet what are seas and what is air? For all
Is God, and but a talisman are heaven and earth
To veil Divinity. For heaven and earth,

Did He not permeate them, were but names;
Know then, that both this visible world and that
Which unseen is, alike are God Himself,
Naught is, save God: and all that is, is God.
And yet, alas! by how few is He seen,
Blind are men's eyes, though all resplendent shines
The world by Deity's own light illumined,
O Thou whom man perceiveth not, although
To him Thou deignest to make known Thyself;
Thou all Creation art, all we behold, but Thou,
The soul within the body lies concealed,
And Thou dost hide Thyself within the soul,
O soul in soul! Myst'ry in myst'ry hid!
Before all wert Thou, and are more than all!

JACOPONE DA TODI

Love That Is Silent

Love, silent as the night,
  Who not one word wilt say,
That none may know thee right!

O Love that lies concealed,
  Through heat and storm and cold,
That none may guess nor read
  Thy secrets manifold;
Lest thieves should soon grow bold
  To steal away thy treasure,
    Snatch it and take to flight!

Deep-hid, thy secret fires
  More ardently shall glow;
And he who screens thee close,
  Thy fiercest heat shall know;

But he who fain would show
Thy mysteries, will be wounded,
Scorched by thy fiery might.

The man who strives to tell
That secret joy within,
In vain he babbles thus:
Before his words begin
The bitter winds of sin
Will storm and whirl around him,
And wreck his treasure bright.

The man who sets his torch
High on a candlestick,
To let it shine in peace,
Shields it with shutters thick,
Lest winds should catch the wick,
Through open casements blowing,
And quench its flick'ring light.

'Tis Silence, at thy door
Holds captive all thy sighs:
Mute Love hath set him there,
He will not let him rise;
So shall thou hold thy prize
That it may live within thee,
Not scattered left and right.

For if thy sighs come forth,
Therewith comes forth thy mind,
To wander far from home,
And leave her joy behind,
Nor can she ever find
The Good, bestowed upon her,
That Treasure Infinite.

Mute Love hath thrust away
False Seeming from his side,
In Love's fair land and realm
No longer to abide.
Hypocrisy and Pride,
And all that do them homage
Are chased to outer night.

Knowledge

Knowledge acquired may contemplate full well,
But ne'er affection set in order right;
Knowledge infused His taste alone can tell,
But in the heart the flame of love can light.
With God it ranges thee,
Thy neighbor edifies,
Thy selfhood vilifies,
And in Truth holds thee free.

SOLOMON IBN-GABIROL

The Royal Crown

Thou existest, but hearing of ear cannot reach Thee, nor vision of eye,
Nor shall the How have sway over Thee, nor the Wherefore and Whence.
Thou existest, but for Thyself and for none other with Thee.
Thou existest, and before Time began Thou wast,
And without place Thou didst abide.
Thou existest, and Thy secret is hidden, and who shall attain to it?
"So deep, so deep, who can discover it?"

Thou livest, but not from any restricted season nor
from any known period.
Thou livest, but not through breath and soul, for Thou
art soul of the soul.
Thou livest, but not with the life of man, which is like
unto vanity and its end the moth and the worm.
Thou livest, and he who layeth hold of Thy secret
"He shall eat and live for ever."

Thou art God, and all things formed are Thy servants
and worshippers.
Yet is not Thy glory diminished by reason of those
that worship aught beside Thee,
For the yearning of them all is to draw nigh Thee,
But they are like the blind,
Setting their faces forward on the King's highway,
Yet still wandering from the path.
One sinketh into the well of a pit,
And another falleth into a snare,
But all imagine they have reached their desire,
Albeit they have suffered in vain.
But Thy servants are those walking clear-eyed in the
straight path,
Turning neither to the right nor the left,
Till they come to the court of the King's palace.
Thou art God, by Thy Godhead sustaining all that
hath been formed,
And upholding in Thy Unity all creatures.
Thou art God, and there is no distinction betwixt Thy
Godhead and Thy Unity, Thy pre-existence and Thy
existence,
For 'tis all one mystery;
And although the name of each be different,
"Yet they are all proceeding to one place."

'IRAQI

That Single Essence

No atom doth exist apart from It,
  that Essence single:
'Tis when Itself doth reveal that first
  those "others" mingle.
O Thou whose outward seeming Lover is,
  Beloved thine Essence,
Who hitherto e'er saw the Object Sought
  seek its own presence?

All Is He

He perfect is alone, and glorious
for evermore, His Unity supreme
above imagining, His wondrous work
beyond analysis. I do not say,
He is the soul's soul: whatsoe'er I say,
that He transcends, for He is free of space,
and may not be attained by swiftest thought
or further sense. Before His essence true
denial, affirmation, both are vain;
Whatever thing is borne by sense to mind
or shaped in fantasy, be all the fruit
or all the mind, all has its life in Him,
nay, all is He. Whatever else but Him
in either world appears is but the double
descried in image by the twisted eye.
His word is first and last: He of creation
outward and inward is. The body's house

is lighted through the spirit's open door
by radiance divine, He is the light
of heaven and earth, His everlasting ray
The Holy Spirit. Whosoe'er has light
within his soul, the ground thereof is light:
within the lantern's glass the niche of night
to radiant morn is turned, and when the soul
sits thus with light, thereafter the heart's steel
contacting it is quickened into flame.
So made the Friend similitude twixt light
and fire, and from that day our lot was cast.
When the Beloved His Face doth show, my sight
augments to vision. Never human eye
hath won pre-excellence above the glance
irradiated by the light of God:
if thou wilt only thine own sight regard,
thine eyes see not, save by the light of God.
If thou wouldst serve the Friend and win His grace,
He is thine eye, thine ear, thy tongue, thy brain;
and since through Him thou speakest, and through Him
hearest, before His Being thou art naught;
for so, when shines the sun's own radiance,
the light of stars is darkened. Never man
of own purpose unto Him hath won,
yet by His power thou canst behold His face!
Though earth may not attain the pure world, soul
shall yet by Soul perceive. The shaft of thought
that silences the shout of alleluia
is honey to the heart, and I am dumb;
I cannot count His praises infinite.

JAMI

Truth Is One

In long devotion to forms that cheat
Thou hast suffered the days of thy life to fleet:
But outward forms are still passing away,
Changing their fashion from day to day.
Tread not ever on stones that are rough to thy feet;
Nor shift from one branch to another thy seat.
Seek high o'er the sphere of the world thy rest;
In the world of reality make thee a nest.
If Truth be thine object, form-worshippers shun;
For form is manifold, Truth is one.
In number trouble and error lie.
To Unity then for sure refuge fly.
If the might of the foeman oppress thee sore,
Fly to the fortress and fear no more.

KABIR

The Formless God

All things are created by the Om;
The love-form is His body.
He is without form, without quality,
  without decay:
Seek thou union with Him!

But that formless God takes a
  thousand forms in the eyes of His
  creatures:

He is pure and indestructible,
His form is infinite and fathomless,
He dances in rapture, and waves of
form arise from His dance.
The body and the mind cannot contain
themselves, when they are touched
by His great joy.
He is immersed in all consciousness,
all joys, and all sorrows;
He has no beginning and no end;
He holds all within His bliss.

LALLESWARI (or LAL DIDDI)

Contemplation

Striving and struggling, for the door was tight
Bolted and barred, till she longed the more
Him to behold that was beyond her sight,
Yet she could not but gaze at the door.

Yet as she stood gazing at the door,
Contemplating Him with all her soul,
Lo! He opened it for ever more:
There, within herself she saw Him whole.
Lalla burnt the foulness from her soul,
Famed abroad, a prophetess was she:
Freed from desire, and her heart made whole,
Knelt she, just there, on her bended knee.

LAO-TZU

Mystic Unity

Those who know do not talk,
And talkers do not know.

Stop your sense,
Close the doors;
Let sharp things be blunted,
Tangles resolved,
The light tempered,
And turmoil subdued;
For this is mystic unity
In which the Wise Man is moved
Neither by affection
Nor yet by estrangement
Or profit or loss
Or honor or shame.
Accordingly, by all the world,
He is held highest.

Divinity Is the Way

Touch ultimate emptiness,
Hold steady and still.

All things work together:
I have watched them reverting,
And have seen how they flourish
And return again, each to his roots.

This, I say, is the stillness:
A retreat to one's roots:
Or better yet, return
To the will of God,
Which is, I say, to constancy;
I call enlightenment, and say
That not to know it
Is blindness that works evil.

But when you know
What eternally is so,
You have stature,
And stature means righteousness,
And righteousness is kingly,
And kingliness divine,
And divinity is the Way
Which is final.

Then, though you die,
You shall not perish.

DHAN GOPAL MUKERJI

Thou Art the Path

Thou art the Path,
And the Goal that paths never reach;
Thou art the Lawful Lord
In Whom laws are lost
Like rivers in the sea.

Thou feedest and sustainest
All that one sees, or seems;
Yet Thou art ever hungry for love,
And there is no end to Thy thirst for peace.

Though all Time is as mail on Thy nakedness;
Though all space sandal thy feet,
Yet they are torn by the thorns of my prayers,
And Thy Body is pierced with bliss.

All-healer, yet all-wounds,
All-life, yet ever-dying,
All-praised, yet praiseless,
All-ending, yet no end for Thee!

Thou art the agony of men,
Thou art the cry of the wounded beast,
Thou art the haughty mountain,
And the eagle swooping down its side.

The unborn that sings under its mother's heart,
The battle-cry of the new-born child;
The song in the throat of the lover,
And the pang of joy that brims in the eye of a bride.

Thou art the curve-pattern that bird-wings
Make in the sky,
Thou art the trembling grass,
And the tiger that creeps under it.

Thou art the dark door of death,
Thou art the anguish of disease,
Thou the fear of the frightened,
And the secret shame of pride.

In the reed the song,
In the string the tune,
Of the drum its beat.

Thou art the taste in water,
Thou art the light in sun and moon,

The sounds fading into Silence,
And the sanctity of sacred Books.

Thou art the diadem of Beauty,
Thou art the crown of Truth,
Thou art the scepter of Reality,
Thou art Good that destroys evil,
And Holiness that vanquishes Good.

NANAK

Naked Wilt Thou Depart

Relish not, O thou, the taste of poison,
O thou foolish and crazy one, thou art involved with the world,
As is the stray cattle let loose upon a farm.
The things thou thinkest are of avail to thee,
Go not with thee; no, not even a trite.
Thou camest naked, naked wilt thou depart.

Thou wert destined to go the Round, and death clasped thee in her grip.
Thou see-est the bloom of the safflower, and thou art lured by its passing fragrance.
And thy string of life wears off each day,
And yet thou doest not a thing to save thy soul.
Thus becometh thou old, thy speech falters and thy body fails thee:
And as thou wert lured by Maya in youth, so verily thou hast remained in age.
When I saw thus the world, through the Guru's grace,
I lost my ego and sought the Lord's refuge.
Yea, Nanak knew then the Path of the Lord through the Saints.

Praise Thou the Truth

In all forms, all colors, art Thou,
Many, O many, are born to die again and again;
Thou alone art the Eternal, Unknowable,
And through the Guru's word art Thou known.
Sacrifice, O Sacrifice am I to the one
Who cherisheth the Lord's Name in his mind;
Yea, He who is beyond form, sign and color,
And who, through the Guru's word, is revealed.
Know ye that in all is the light of the One alone.
And by the service of the Guru doth He become manifest.
He alone is the manifest all over; unmanifest is He too;
Yea, in His light is our light merged.

The world is being burnt by the fire of desire,
And greed and abundance of ego;
It cometh and goeth and loseth Honor,
And loseth its life in vain.
Rare is the one who knoweth the Guru's word,
Then he dies not again, and merges in the Truth the natural way.
He fixes not his mind then on Maya,
And, through the Guru's word, he mergeth ever (in the Lord);
And he praiseth the All-pervading Lord,
And, on Truth, he seemeth Beauteous.
Praise thou the True One, the Eternal Presence,
Who permeates the Guru's word through and through;
By the Guru's grace is His Truth revealed and yea,
one gathereth Bliss through Truth.

The Truth abideth forever in the mind,
The Truth is ever Eternal; it cometh nor goeth;
They who take to the Truth are forever pure in mind,
And through the Guru's word merge they in the Truth.
Praise thou the Truth, and nought else,
By serving which one getteth Eternal peace. . . .

JACOB REVIUS

The Knowledge of God

When starlight shines on the surface of the sea,
The fishes underneath do all agree,
And think that there the stars of Heaven show,
Although reflection scant is all they know;
But we who here above the water live
Can see the bright hosts of the night arrive.
So Man: all that he sees on earth this while,
Of God and of his glory, is not real:
'Tis image mere; who naked truth can bear,
They only see God's shining visage clear.

RUMI

Fons Vitae

Poor copies out of Heaven's original,
Pale earthly pictures moldering to decay,
What care although your beauties break and fall,
When that which gave them life endures for aye?

Oh, never vex thine heart with idle woes:
All high discourse enchanting the rapt ear,
All gilded landscapes and brave glistering shows
Fade—perish, but it is not as we fear.

Whilst far away the living fountains ply,
Each petty brook goes brimful to the main.
Since brook nor fountain can forever die,
Thy fears how foolish, thy lament how vain!

What is this fountain, wouldst thou rightly know?
The Soul whence issue all created things.
Doubtless the rivers shall not cease to flow
Till silenced are the everlasting springs.

Farewell to sorrow, and with quiet mind
Drink long and deep: let others fondly deem
The channel empty they perchance may find,
Or fathom that unfathomable stream.

The moment thou to this low world wast given,
A ladder stood whereby thou mightst aspire;
And first thy steps, which upward still have striven,
From mineral mounted to the plant; then higher.

To animal existence; next, the Man
With knowledge, reason, faith. O wondrous goal!
This body, which a crumb of dust began—
How fairly fashioned the consummate whole!

Yet stay not here thy journey: thou shalt grow
An angel bright and have thine home in Heaven.
Plod on, plunge last in the great Sea, that so
Thy little drop make oceans seven times seven.

"The Son of God!" Nay, leave that word unsaid;
Say, "God is One, the pure, the single Truth."
What though thy frame be withered, old, and dead,
If the soul keep her fresh immortal youth?

ANGELUS SILESIUS

Contemplation

You will have heav'n on earth,
The sweetest life to live,
If you yourself with love
To contemplation give.

God Mine End

God is my final end;
Does He from me evolve,
Then He grows out of me
While I in Him dissolve.

SWAMI VIVEKANANDA

The Living God

He who is in you and outside you,
Who works through all hands,
Who walks on all feet,
Whose body are all ye,
Him worship, and break all other idols!

He who is at once the high and low,
The sinner and the saint,
Both God and worm,
Him worship—visible, knowable, real, omnipresent,
Break all other idols!

In whom is neither past life
Nor future birth nor death,
In whom we always have been
And always shall be one,
Him worship. Break all other idols!

Ye fools! Who neglect the living God,
And His infinite reflections with which the world is full,
While ye run after imaginary shadows,
That lead alone to fights and quarrels,
Him worship, the only visible!
Break all other idols!

To a Friend

Where darkness is interpreted as light,
Where misery passes for happiness,
Where disease is pretended to be health,
Where the new-born's cry but shows 'tis alive;
Dost thou, O wise, expect happiness here?

Where war and competition ceaseless run,
Even the father turns against the son,
Where "self, self"—this always the only note,
Dost thou, O wise, seek for peace supreme here?

A glaring mixture of heaven and hell,
Who can fly from this Samsâr of Mâyâ?
Fastened in the neck with Karma's fetters,
Say, where can the slave escape for safety?

The paths of Yoga and of sense-enjoyment,
The life of the householder and Sannyâs,
Devotion, worship and earning riches,

Vows, Tyâga and austerities severe,
I have seen through them all. What have I known?

—Have known there's not a jot of happiness,
Life is only a cup of Tantalus;*
The nobler is your heart, know for certain,
The more must be your share of misery.

Thou large-hearted Lover unselfish, know,
There's no room in this sordid world for thee;
Can a marble figure e'er brook the blow
That an iron mass can afford to bear?

Couldst thou be as one inert and abject,
Honey-mouthed, but with poison in thy heart,
Destitute of truth and worshipping self,
Then thou wouldst have a place in this Samsâr.

Pledging even life for gaining knowledge,
I have devoted half my days on earth
For the sake of love, ev'n as one insane,
I have often clutched at shadows lifeless;

For religion many creeds have I sought,
Lived in mountain-caves, on cremation grounds,
By the Ganges and other sacred streams,
And how many days have I passed on alms!

* A scientific toy consisting of a cup with a puppet in its bowl. Water may be poured into the bowl as high as the puppet's chin, and then it will recede, being let out at the bottom through a siphon concealed in the puppet's body. (Tantalus, a wealthy king and son of Zeus, was punished in the lower world by being condemned to stand in water up to the chin and beneath fruit-laden branches, with water and fruit receding at each attempt to drink or eat.)

Friendless, clad in rags, with no possession,
Feeding from door to door on what chance would bring,
The frame broken under Tapasyâ's weight;
What riches, ask thou, have I earned in life?

Listen, friend, I will speak my heart to thee,
I have found in my life this truth supreme,
Buffeted by waves, in this whirl of life,
There's one ferry that takes across the sea.*

Formulas of worship, control of breath,
Science, philosophy, systems varied,
Relinquishment, possession, and the like,
All these are but delusions of the mind;
Love, Love—that's the one thing, the sole treasure.

In Jiva and Brahman, in man and God,
In ghosts and wraiths and spirits and so forth,
In Devas, beasts, birds, insects, and in worms,
This Prema dwells in the heart of them all.

Say, who else is the highest God of gods?
Say, who else moves all the universe?
The mother dies for her young, robber robs!
Both are but the impulse of the same Love!

Beyond the ken of human speech and mind,
It dwells in weal and woe; 'Tis that which comes,
As the all-powerful, all-destroyer
Kali, and as the kindliest mother.

Disease, bereavement, pinch of poverty,
Dharma, and its opposite Adharma,
The results of actions good and bad, all

* Sea of Samsara.

Are but ITS worship in manifold modes;
Say, who does by himself a Jiva do?

Deluded is he who happiness seeks,
Lunatic he who misery wishes,
Insane he too who fondly longs for death,
Immortality—vain aspiration!

Far, far, however far you may travel,
Mounted on the brilliant mental car,
'Tis the same ocean of the Samsâr,
Happiness and misery whirling on.

Listen, O Vihangam,* bereft of wings,
'Tis not the way to make good your escape;
Time and again you get blows, and collapse,
Why then attempt what is impossible?

Let go your vain reliance on knowledge,
Let go your prayers, offerings and strength,
For Love selfless is the only resource;
Lo, the insects teach—embracing the flame.

The base insect's blind, by beauty charmed.
Thy soul is drunken with the wine of Love;
O thou Lover true, cast into the fire
All thy dross of self, thy mean selfishness.

Say—comes happiness e'er to a beggar?
What good being object of charity?
Give away, ne'er turn to ask in return,
Should there be the wealth treasured in thy heart.

* Bird; here addressed to the bound soul.

Aye, born heir to the Infinite thou art,
Within the heart is the ocean of Love,
"Give," "Give away"—whoever asks return,
His ocean dwindles down to a mere drop.

From the highest Brahman to the yonder worm,
And to the very minutest atom,
Everywhere is the same God, the All-Love;
Friend, offer mind, soul, body, at their feet.

These are His manifold forms before thee,
Rejecting them, where seekest thou for God?

Who loves all beings, without distinction,
He indeed is worshipping best his God.

5. Divine Ecstasy

THE LOVE OF INTOXICATION, RAPTURE, AND BLISS.

ANONYMOUS

Tears of Joy

When I behold Thy peerless face, beaming with love, O Lord,
What fear have I of earthly woe or of the frown of sorrow?
As the first ray of the dawning sun dispels the dark,
So too, Lord, when Thy blessed light bursts forth within the heart,
It scatters all our grief and pain with sweetest balm.
When on Thy love and grace I ponder, in my heart's deepest
depths,
Tears of joy stream down my cheeks beyond restraining.
Hail, Gracious Lord! Hail, Gracious One! I shall proclaim Thy
love.
May my life-breath depart from me as I perform Thy works!

Blissful Awareness

Upon the Sea of Blissful Awareness waves of ecstatic love arise:
Rapture divine! Play of God's Bliss!
Oh, how enthralling!
Wondrous waves of the sweetness of God, ever new and ever
enchanting,
Rise on the surface, ever assuming
Forms ever fresh.

Then once more in the Great Communion all are merged,
as the barrier walls
of time and space dissolve and vanish:

Dance then, O mind!
Dance in delight, with hands upraised, chanting Lord Hari's*
holy name.

JACOPONE DA TODI

Sing for Very Love

Thou, Jubilus, the heart dost move;
And makest us sing for very love.

The Jubilus in fire awakes,
And straight the man must sing and pray;
His tongue in childish stammering shakes,
Nor knows he what his lips may say;
He cannot quench nor hide away
That Sweetness pure and infinite.

The Jubilus in flame is lit,
And straight the man must shout and sing;
So close to Love his heart is knit,
He scarce can bear the honeyed sting;
His clamor and his cries must ring,
And shame forever take to flight.

The Jubilus enslaves man's heart
—A love-bewildered prisoner—
And see! his neighbors stand apart,

* Name of God in His Personal aspect.

And mock the senseless chatterer:
They deem his speech a foolish blur,
A shadow of his spirit's light.

Yea, when thou enterest the mind,
O Jubilus, thou rapture fair,
The heart of man new skill doth find
Love's own disguise to grasp and wear,
The suffering of Love to bear,
With song and clamor of delight!

And thus the uninitiate
Will deem that thou art crazed indeed;
They see thy strange and fevered state,
But have not wit thy heart to read;
Within, deep-pierced, that heart may bleed,
Hidden from curious mortal sight.

Rapture Divine

When the mind's very being is gone,
Sunk in a conscious sleep,
In a rapture divine and deep,
Itself in the Godhead lost:
It is conquered, ravished, and won!
Set in Eternity's sweep,
Gazing back on the steep,
Knowing not how it was crossed—
To a new world now it is tossed,
Drawn from its former state,
To another, measureless, great,
Where Love is drowned in the Sea.

O Gentle Love

O Gentle Love,
Who died for Love,
I pray Thee, slay me for Love!

Love, Who didst lead
To death indeed,
Thy Lover upon the Cross,
O tell me why
Thy Dear must die?
—'Twas to redeem my loss.
Then try me by fire,
For 'tis all my desire
To die in the arms of Love.

If Thou didst not spare
Thy Beloved there;
How should I escape from Thee?
Thy Love hath took
Me with an hook,
Thy fish from out of the sea:
Then spare me not,
For 'tis all my thought
To perish, immersed in Love.

. . .

O Love of the Lamb;
O Ocean calm!
Of thy depths what tongue can tell?
In Thee am I drowned,
For Above and Around,
Thy fathomless waters well!
And the straightest road,
To the Heart of God,
Is the Swirl and the Folly of Love.

O Love Divine

O Love divine, and Lord,
That asks for no reward!

O Love, O Love, Thy tender amity
Is full of joy and gladness,
And into grief and sadness
That heart shall never fall that tasteth Thee.

O Love, O Love, Thou dearest art and best:
Love that with fire consumes,
Yet safeguards and illumes
The heart that houseth Thee, beloved Guest.

Dulcet as honeyed stings those wounds must be,
Sweet wounds of rapture bright,
All joy, and all delight—
The wounds of him whose heart is pierced by Thee!

Love, Thou didst enter very softly in
To hold this heart of mine.
No sound, no stir, no sign!
How couldst Thou cross my threshold all unseen!

O Love adorable, with sweetness fraught,
O Love delectable,
Love inconceivable,
Outstripping knowledge and surpassing thought!

O Love, Thou fire divine, of laughter spun;
Love, that art smile and jest,
Thou giv'st us of Thy best,
Thy wealth unmeasured that is never done.

. . .

Science is vain, and knowledge but a cheat:
He who by learning's skill
Would hold Thee at his will,
His heart shall never taste Thy savor sweet.

For store of science is a deadly dart;
'Twill slay herself at length,
Save if she clothe her strength
In the fair garment of an humble heart.

. . .

O Love, forever glowing and aflame,
Kindle Thy warriors' hearts,
And turn their tongues to darts,
To pierce each soul that hears Thy sacred name.

. . .

Love, Giver of light to all that fain would shine,
Thy light alone is bright,
There beams none other light,
Save with a sullen glow that is not Thine.

Thou light, so vivid and so luminous,
Thy lover cannot know
Pure radiance, steadfast glow,
Save in Thy rays, that lighten all of us.

O Love, Thy keen and piercing brilliancy
Illumes and guides the mind,
That Object fair to find—
The end and aim of all her fervency.

O Love, Thine ardors pure and passionate
Wake and inflame the heart,
To dwell no more apart,
With the Adored made One and incarnate.

Love, Thou art life, in certain safety set,
Eternal art Thou there;
Thou'rt wealth, unspoilt by care,
And measureless beyond our utmost debt.

. . .

Love, it was Thou Thyself that didst inspire
My heart to love Thee first;
—Ahungered and athirst,
Thy love longed, with very great desire.

'IRAQI

We Yield Our Hearts

Lodgers we who on Thy threshold dwell,
and nightingales that in Thy garden sing,
whether we leave Thy door, or waiting stand,
of only Thee we speak, of Thee we hear.
Since we are captives caught within Thy nets,
where shall we trust our passion or our heads?
And since in Thy affection we draw breath,
how shall we yearn for strangers? Lo, we lay
our heads upon the threshold of Thy door,
waiting to come to Thee. Since we have quaffed
the beaker of Thy love, we yield our hearts
and make our lives Thy ransom; since we come
again into Thy street, we turn our backs
on all that is, save Thee. Our souls are bound
to serve Thee, though in grief, and we have died
to selfhood! We are captives of Thy love
and have not strength to flee. Thy beauty's fever
hath lit a flame: shall not our hearts be burned?

When in Love's Snare

When in love's snare the soul doth lie
  it is no sin for eye to see:
though far Thy face from outward eye,
  with inward sight I gaze on Thee.

My soul is drunken with the wine
  quaffed on that first primeval day
when Thou wast mine, and I was Thine,
  and promised so to be for aye.

I cannot let my Lover go,
  though I am doomed to banishment:
the spark betrays the ember's glow,
  this blush, my soul's bewilderment.

Thy languorous eye is lover's bane,
  the earth Thou treadest, China's throne:
whate'er Thou willest, Thou dost reign,
  and humbly I obedience own.

ST. JOHN OF THE CROSS

An Ecstasy of High Exaltation

I entered in, I know not where,
And I remained, though knowing naught,
Transcending knowledge with my thought.

Of when I entered I know naught,
But when I saw that I was there
(Though where it was I did not care).
Strange things I learned, with greatness fraught.

Yet what I heard I'll not declare.
But there I stayed, though knowing naught,
Transcending knowledge with my thought.

Of peace and piety interwound
This perfect science had been wrought,
Within the solitude profound
A straight and narrow path it taught,
Such secret wisdom there I found
That there I stammered, saying naught,
But topped all knowledge with my thought.

So borne aloft, so drunken-reeling,
So rapt was I, so swept away,
Within the scope of sense or feeling
My sense or feeling could not stay.
And in my soul I felt, revealing,
A sense that, though its sense was naught,
Transcending knowledge with my thought.

The man who truly there has come
Of his own self must shed the guise;
Of all he knew before the sum
Seems far beneath that wondrous prize:
And in this lore he grows so wise
That he remains, though knowing naught,
Transcending knowledge with his thought.

The farther that I climbed the height
The less I seemed to understand
The cloud so tenebrous and grand
That there illuminates the night.
For he who understands that sight
Remains for aye, though knowing naught,
Transcending knowledge with his thought.

This wisdom without understanding
Is of so absolute a force
No wise man of whatever standing
Can ever stand against its course,
Unless they tap its wondrous source,
To know so much, though knowing naught,
They pass all knowledge with their thought.

This summit all so steeply towers
And is of excellence so high,
No human faculties or powers
Can ever to the top come nigh.
Whoever with its steep could vie,
Though knowing nothing, would transcend
All thought, forever, without end.

If you would ask, what is its essence—
This summit of all sense and knowing:
It comes from the Divinest Presence—
The sudden sense of Him outflowing,
In His great clemency bestowing
The gift that leaves men knowing naught,
Yet passing knowledge with their thought.

LUIS DE LEON

In Rapture Sweet

Through sea of melody
In rapture sweet the soul doth onward glide,
And sinks there finally,
Until whate'er betide
Beyond it to its senses is denied.

O heavenly ravishment!
Life-giving death, oblivion's sweet defense!
O might my life be spent
In thy calm rest, nor thence
Ever return to this vile earthly sense!

To share such bliss I entreat
You, glory of Apollo's sacred choir,
O friend for whom doth beat
My heart beyond desire
Of treasures that bring tears and sorrow dire.

MANIKKAVACHAGAR

Billows of His Bliss

Neither can I drink Thy bliss and thus rest satisfied,
Nor have I the strength to quaff it in.
My heart resembling boist'rous sea on full moon night
He has made like luscious, cooling sea of milk,
And did fill in brimful with the billows of His bliss.
With the flood of sweet ambrosis well beyond all words
He did fill the interstices of my hair-cells full.
This frame of dog-like me He made His 'bode,
Irrigating ev'ry fleshy limb of this body
Of my coarse and cruel self with His grace-like honey.
And with full and wondrous sweet
Ambrosial driblets did He charge
Ev'ry bone's deep pore of mine.
Just as if a body had been made
Out of melting heart alone, He gave
Me a frame wherein does nectar spring.
Even me like Tusker fond of canes
He has blessed with being endless true.

While His mercy's supreme honey
Had been blended within me,
He whose greatness is unknown
Both to Mall and Brahman
Has prepared and served His good
Grace and His ambrosial food.

MIRA BAI

Thou Entwined My Heart

With the twine of His mercy hath He,
O Mother! entwined my heart!
The sharp arrow of His Love,
O Mother! hath pierced me, through and through!
When did the arrow strike me?
I know not! I only know
I cannot endure it now.

O Mother! drugs and charms have I with me,
But pain departeth not!
Who will treat me? Who?
O, the agony of the arrow!

Come quick, my Master!
Come! Be Thou not far!
Come quick to meet me, Lord!

Mighty art Thou, O Mountain-mover!
And ever compassionate art Thou!
With the twine of Thy mercy
Hath Thou entwined my heart,
O Thou of the Lotus-Eyes!

NI'MAT-ALLAH

The Light of His Presence

Last night in a dream I saw the phantom image of his face;
I saw that drunkenly he was drawing me towards him.
With a hundred coquetries the Christian child embraced me—
his waist was bound with a girdle, his hair was flowing free.
My love has the breath of Jesus, bringing new life to my heart;
with whomsoever I speak now, my conversation is of him.
The world has become irradiated by the light of his presence;
sweet-scented grows the earth from his musk-perfumed tresses.
The darling's love is a treasure, seek it in the heart's recess.
Saki, bring wine, and pour it over the crown of my head;
of your kindness wash this robe that wraps about my breast.
Like the ecstatic nightingale I fell upon the rose's face;
for love of Ni'mat Allah he laid his cheek upon mine.

RABI'A

None Beside Thee

O my Joy and my Desire and my Refuge,
My Friend and my Sustainer and my Goal,
Thou art my Intimate, and longing for Thee sustains me.
Were it not for Thee, O my Life and my Friend,
How I should have been distraught over the spaces of the earth.
How many favors have been bestowed, and how much hast
Thou given me.
Of gifts and grace and assistance,
Thy love is now my desire and my bliss,
And has been revealed to the eye of my heart that was athirst.
I have none beside Thee, Who dost make the desert blossom.

Thou art my joy, firmly established within me,
If Thou art satisfied with me, then
O Desire of my heart, my happiness has appeared.

RUMI

Crowned With Eternal Flame

He comes, a Moon whose like the sky ne'er saw,
awake or dreaming,
Crowned with eternal flame no flood can lay.
Lo, from the flagon of Thy love, O Lord, my soul
is swimming,
And ruined all my body's house of clay.

When first the Giver of the grape my lonely heart
befriended,
Wine fired my bosom and my veins filled up;
But when His image all my eye possessed, a voice
descended:
"Well done, O sovereign Wine and peerless Cup!"

Love's mighty arm from roof to base each dark
abode is hewing
Where chinks reluctant catch a golden ray.
My heart, when Love's sea of a sudden burst into
its viewing,
Leaped headlong in, with "Find me now who may!"

As the sun moving, clouds behind him run,
All hearts attend thee, O Tabriz's Sun!

The Shepherd's Prayer

Moses saw a shepherd on the way, crying, "O Lord Who choosest as Thou wilt,
Where art Thou, that I may serve Thee and sew Thy shoon and comb Thy hair?
That I may wash Thy clothes and kill Thy lice and bring milk to Thee, O Worshipful One!
That I may kiss Thy little hand and rub Thy little feet and sweep Thy little room at bed-time."
On hearing these foolish words, Moses said, "Man, to whom are you speaking?
What babble! What blasphemy and raving! Stuff some cotton into your mouth!
Truly the friendship of a fool is enmity: the High God is not in want of suchlike service."
The shepherd rent his garment, heaved a sigh, and took his way to the wilderness.

Then came to Moses a revelation: "Thou has parted My servant from Me.
Wert thou sent as a prophet to unite, or wert thou sent to sever?
I have bestowed on every one a particular mode of worship,
I have given every one a peculiar form of expression.
The idiom of Hindustan is excellent for Hindus; the idiom of Sind is excellent for the people of Sind.

"I look not at tongue and speech, I look at the spirit and the inward feeling.
I look into the heart to see whether it be lowly, though the words uttered be not lowly.
Enough of phrases and conceits and metaphors! I want burning, burning: become familiar with that burning!

Light up a fire of love in thy soul, burn all thought and expression away!
O Moses, they that know the conventions are of one sort, they whose souls burn are of another."

The religion of love is apart from all religions. The lovers of God have no religion but God alone.

SANA'I

Snare of Love

Since my heart was caught in the snare of love,
since my soul became wine in the cup of love,
ah, the pains I have known through loverhood,
since, like a hawk, I fell in the snare of love!
Trapped in time, I am turned to a drunken sot
by the exciting, dreg-draining cup of love.

Dreading the fierce affliction of loverhood,
I dare not utter the very name of love;
and the more amazing is this, since I see
every creature on earth is at peace with love.
"Yield up your soul, your faith, your heart to me"—
so I hear in my soul the message of love:
my soul, my faith, my heart—I surrender all,
so at last to attain my desire of love.*

* Sana'i uses the imagery of love and wine to express his spiritual raptures.

6. *Light of the Soul*

THE LOVE OF ILLUMINATION, ETERNAL LIGHT, AND PEACE

ANONYMOUS
(*Sikh poem on Simran*)

Fibres of Light

I do not know why, but when I say "Hail, Master!"
the sun and stars seem to run in my breath,
my muscles are as if fibres of light,
my being flies to strange lands and waters,
my lips touch gardens of flowers, my hands I exchange with some other hands,
a stranger moves my tongue.
The Universe runs into me, and I into the Universe.
I seem a strange misty form. Like vapor I pass into the being of others, and they passing within me become my guests.
It seems fair forms of rolling beauty roll as waves on the sea—Hail, Lord! All are each other's!
Our shape and limbs run into each other.
I find my bones at times strike within me against the bones of someone else.
Our deeds and thoughts jostle and run into each other.
I see a hundred souls blend in me, and I interchange my blood and brain thus with a hundred more in a single breath; and, calm in solitude, I find a society.

BABA KUHI
(of Shiraz)

Only God I Saw

In the market, in the cloister—only God I saw.
In the valley and on the mountain—only God I saw.
Him I have seen beside me oft in tribulation;
In favor and in fortune—only God I saw.
In prayer and fasting, in praise and contemplation,
In the religion of the Prophet—only God I saw.
Neither soul nor body, accident nor substance,
Qualities nor causes—only God I saw.
I oped mine eyes, and by the light of His Face around me
In all the eye discovered—only God I saw.

Like a candle I was melting in His fire:
Amidst the flames outflanking—only God I saw.
Myself with mine own eyes I saw most clearly,
But when I looked with God's eyes—only God I saw.
I passed away into nothingness, I vanished.
And lo, I was the All-living—only God I saw.

'IRAQI

Light of the World

Light of the world, without thy loveliness
the eye of lover cannot see the day,
nor ever lover's foot aspire to press
love's palace gate, till self is cast away.

No house-bred craven ever dared to know
  within love's wilderness a way to take;
but I—I have been intimate with woe
  that melts the soul, until the heart doth break.

Love said to me: "Go, rend thy rich brocade!
  Tell not thy story, but my tale recite:
put out the flame by thine own passion made,
  and kindle at my love a quenchless light."

ST. JOHN OF THE CROSS

Song of the Soul in Love

Oh flame of love so living,
How tenderly you force
To my soul's inmost core your fiery probe!
Since now you've no misgiving,
End it, pursue your course,
And for our sweet encounter tear the robe!

Oh cautery most tender!
Oh gash that is my guerdon!
Oh gentle hand! Oh touch how softly thrilling!
Eternal life you render,
Raise of all debts the burden
And change my death to life, even while killing!

Oh lamps of fiery blaze
To whose refulgent fuel
The deepest caverns of my soul grow bright,
Late blind with gloom and haze,
But in this strange renewal
Giving to the belov'd both heat and light.

What peace, with love enwreathing,
You conjure to my breast,
Which only you your dwelling place may call:
While with delicious breathings
In glory, grace, and rest,
So daintily in love you make me fall!

Songs of the Soul in Rapture

Upon a gloomy night,
With all my cares to loving ardors flushed,
(O venture of delight!)
With nobody in sight
I went abroad when all my house was hushed.

In safety, in disguise,
In darkness up the secret stair I crept,
(O happy enterprise)
Concealed from other eyes
When all my house at length in silence slept.

Upon that lucky night
In secrecy, inscrutable to sight,
I went without discerning
And with no other light
Except for that which in my heart was burning.

It lit and led me through
More certain than the light of noonday clear
To where One waited near
Whose presence well I knew,
There where no other presence might appear.

Oh night that was my guide!
Oh darkness dearer than the morning's pride,
Oh night that joined the lover
To the beloved bride,
Transfiguring them each into the other.

Within my flowering breast,
Which only for himself entire I save,
He sank into his rest,
And all my gifts I gave,
Lulled by the airs with which the cedars wave.

Over the ramparts fanned,
While the fresh wind was fluttering his tresses,
With his serenest hand
My neck he wounded, and
Suspended every sense with its caresses.

Lost to myself, I stayed,
My face upon my lover having laid,
From all endeavor ceasing:
And all my cares releasing,
Threw them amongst the lilies there to fade.

KABIR

The Music That Transcends All

The Lord is in me, the Lord is in you,
as life is in every seed. O servant!
put false pride away, and seek for
Him within you.

A million suns are ablaze with light,
The sea of blue spreads in the sky,
The fever of life is stilled, and all
stains are washed away; when
I sit in the midst of that world.

Hark to the unstruck bells and drums!
Take your delight in love!
Rains pour down without water, and
the rivers are streams of light.
One Love it is that pervades the whole
world, few there are who know it fully:
They are blind who hope to see it by
the light of reason, that reason
which is the cause of separation—
The House of Reason is very far away!

How blessed is Kabir, that amidst
this great joy he sings within his
own vessel.
It is the music of the meeting of soul
with soul;
It is the music of the forgetting of
sorrows;
It is the music that transcends all
coming in and all going forth.

Love's Perfection

Beneath the great umbrella of my
King millions of suns and moons
and stars are shining!
He is the Mind within my mind: He
is the Eye within mine eye.

Ah, could my mind and eyes be one!
  Could my love but reach to my
  Lover! Could but the fiery heart
  of my heart be cooled!
Kabir says: "When you unite love
  with the Lover, then you have
  love's perfection."

LUIS DE LEON

A New Light Doth Shine

At whose blest sound divine
My soul that in forgetfulness hath lain
  With a new light doth shine
And unto memory plain
  Of its first splendid origin attain.

Up through the fields of air
It wings, till in the highest sphere it dwells
And a new music there
It hears, music that wells
Undying, and all other kinds excels.

MECHTHILD OF MAGDEBURG

Love Flows From God

Love flows from God to man without effort
As a bird glides through the air
Without moving its wings—
Thus they go whithersoever they will
United in body and soul

Yet in their form separate—
  As the Godhead strikes the note
Humanity sings,
The Holy Spirit is the harpist
And all the strings must sound
Which are strung in love.

Light of Splendor

With the dull hearing of my misery—
A light of utmost splendor
Glows on the eyes of my soul.
Therein have I seen the inexpressible ordering
Of all things, and recognized God's unspeakable glory—
That incomprehensible wonder—
The tender caress between God and the soul,
The sufficiency in the Highest,
Discipline in understanding,
Realization with withdrawal,
According to the power of the senses,
The unmingled joy of union,
The living love of Eternity
As it now is and evermore shall be.

MIRA BAI

O Eternal Light!

In Thee, Beloved, is Light:
And the Light doth shine
In darkness of the world,
And the world knows it not!
O Light! Eternal Light!

With a million eyes dost Thou
Fill all worlds, all stars and suns.
With a mercy immeasurable
Dost Thou shine on me—
A pilgrim through endless space
To Thy Holy Shrine!

Torch of Light

I love Thee, Shyama!
I love Thee more than life!
My strength, my solace and my bliss
In Thee alone I find—
In Thee and Thy Holy Name—
My sweetest one!

When all is dark
Thy Name awakes in me a Light!
It burneth as a Flame
In my heart: day and night
It shines before me
As a Torch of Light,
Beautiful and bright!

RABI'A

Peace in Solitude

My peace, O my brothers, is in solitude,
And my Beloved is with me always.
For His love I can find no substitute,
And His love is the test for me among mortal beings,
Whene'er His Beauty I may contemplate;
He is my "mihrab"; towards Him is my "qibla."

If I die of love, before completing satisfaction,
Alas, for my anxiety in the world, alas for my distress.
O Healer (of souls), the heart feeds upon its desire;
The striving after union with Thee has healed my soul.
O my Joy and my Life abidingly,
Thou wast the source of my life and from Thee also came
my ecstasy.
I have separated myself from all created beings,
My hope is for union with Thee, for that is the goal
of my desire.

ANGELUS SILESIUS

One With God

God is in me the fire
And I beam of his light.
Thus we together are
And closely we unite.

Ray of His Light

Am not outside of God
Nor He outside of me!
Am His effulgent light;
Source of my glory He.

Be Like Him

God is eternal rest,
For naught e'er willeth He.
If naught thou willest, thou
As much as God shalt be.

SISUPACALA

On Fire Is All the World

On fire is all the world, is all in flames!
A blaze is all the world, the heav'ns do quake!
But that which quaketh not, that ever sure,
That priceless thing, unheeded by the world,
Even the Norm—*that* hath the Buddha taught
To me, therein my mind delighted dwells.
And I who heard his blessed word abide
Fain only and always to do his will.
The Threefold Wisdom have I gotten now,
And done the bidding of the Buddha blest.
On every hand the love of sense is slain
And the thick gloom of ignorance is rent
In twain. Know this, O Evil One, avaunt!
Here, O Destroyer, shalt thou not prevail!

SUJATA

The Ambrosial Path

Him saw I sitting there, Light of the World,
And went into his presence worshipping.
And of his great compassion for us all,
He taught to me the Norm—the One who Sees!

Forthwith I, too, could pierce and penetrate,
Hearing the truth taught by the mighty Seer.
For there, e'en as I sat, my spirit touched
The Norm Immaculate, the Ambrosial Path.

Then first it was I left the life of home,
When the blest Gospel I had come to know,
And now the Threefold Wisdom have I won.
O wise and sure the bidding of the Lord!

SUNDARI-NANDA

The Peace of Nibbana

I, even I, have seen, inside and out,
This body as in truth it really is,
Who sought to know the "what" and "why"
With zeal unfaltering and ardor fired.
Now for the body care I never more,
And all my consciousness is passion-free.
Keen with unfettered zeal, detached,
Calm and serene, I taste Nibbana's peace.

SWAMI VIVEKANANDA

Peace

Behold, it comes in night,
The power that is not power,
The light that is in darkness,
The shade in dazzling light.

It is joy that never spoke,
And grief unfelt, profound,
Immortal life unlived,
Eternal death unmourned.

It is not joy nor sorrow,
But that which is between,
It is not night nor morrow,
But that which joins them in.

It is sweet rest in music,
And pause in sacred art,
The silence between speaking;
Between two fits of passion—
It is the calm of heart.

It is beauty never seen,
And love that stands alone,
It is song that lives unsung,
And knowledge never known.

It is death between two lives,
And lull between two storms,
The void whence rose creation,
And that where it returns.

To it the tear-drop goes,
To spread the smiling form.
It is the Goal of Life,
And Peace—its only home!

7. The Joy of Surrender

THE LOVE OF SACRIFICE

ABSORPTION, AND UNION

ANONYMOUS

Immerse Yourself for Evermore

Meditate, O my mind, on the Lord,
The Stainless One, Pure Spirit through and through.
How peerless is the light that in Him shines!
How soul-bewitching is His wondrous form!
How dear is He to all His devotees!

Ever more beauteous in fresh-blossoming love
That shames the splendor of a million moons,
Like lightning gleams the glory of His form,
Raising erect the hair for very joy.

Worship His feet in the lotus of your heart;
With mind serene and eyes made radiant
With heavenly love, behold that matchless sight.
Caught in the spell of His love's ecstasy,
Immerse yourself for evermore, O mind,
In Him who is Pure Knowledge and Pure Bliss.

'ATTAR

I Vanished

As from myself I vanished,
  In self I passed from view:
A dewdrop came from Ocean,
  In ocean drowned the dew.

At first I was a shadow,
  On earth obscurely cast:
The Sun shone forth in splendor,
  And so from view I passed.

Of coming is no token,
  Of parting tale is none;
My coming and my parting
  Were but a moment gone.

O ask of me no tiding,
  For mothlike in the fire
Of the Beloved's beauty
  I perished in desire.

Upon this path of passion
  Set foot, if thou art wise:
In love I lacked all knowledge
  And all did realize.

My body all was vision,
  Yet I was wholly blind:—
This seeing-and-unseeing
  O wonderful to find!

Dust be upon my temples,
  If in the least I know
Whither in wild distraction
  This heart of mine did go.

When 'Attar's heart transcending
  Both worlds I did descry,
Moved by his heart's emotion
  Distraught of heart was I.

JACOPONE DA TODI

The Highest Wisdom

Wisdom 'tis and courtesy,
Crazed for Jesus Christ to be.

No such learning can be found
In Paris, nor the world around;
In this folly to abound
  Is the best philosophy.

Who by Christ is all possessed,
Seems afflicted and distressed,
Yet is Master of the best,
  In science and theology.

Who for Christ is all distraught,
Gives his wits, men say, for naught;
—Those whom Love hath never taught,
  Deem he erreth utterly.

He who enters in this school,
Learns a new and wondrous rule:
"Who hath never been a fool,
  Wisdom's scholar cannot be."

He who enters on this dance,
Enters Love's unwalled expanse;
—Those who mock and look askance,
  Should do penance certainly.

He that worldly praise achieves,
Jesus Christ his Savior grieves,
Who, Himself, between two thieves,
  On the Cross hung patiently.

He that seeks for shame and pain,
Shall his heart's desire attain:
All Bologna's lore were vain,
  To increase his mastery.

The Soul's Over-Ardent Love

Love, that art Charity,
Why hast Thou hurt me so?
My heart is smote in two,
And burns with ardent love.
Glowing and flaming, refuge finding none,
My heart is fettered fast, it cannot flee;
It is consumed, like wax set in the sun;
  Living, yet dying, swooning passionately,
It prays for strength a little way to run,
  Yet in this furnace must it bide and be:
  Where am I led, ah me!

To depths so high?
Living I die,
So fierce the fire of Love.

. . .

All that I had, to purchase Love I gave,
Yea, Love hath ruined me,
All crazed my thought;
I am sold for naught,
Beggared and stript by Love.

. . .

Now are we one, we are not separate;
Fire cannot part us, nor a sword divide;
Not pain nor death can reach these heights so great
Where Love hath snatched and set me by His side:
Far, far below, I see the worlds gyrate,
Far, far above, my heart is satisfied:
My soul, who is thy Guide
To this strange bliss?
'Tis Jesu's kiss,
All sweetness far above.

Now on no creature can I turn my sight,
But on my Maker all my mind is set;
Earth, sea, and sky are emptied of delight,
For Christ's dear love all else I clean forget:
Cherubim, seraphim, in who are met
Wisdom and Love, must yet
Give place, give place
To that One Face
To my dear Lord of Love.

. . .

For heaven and earth and all things else do cry,
That Love is all my task, my life, my place;

Their heartfelt voices cry aloud—"Draw nigh!
  The Love that made thee, hasten to embrace!
That Love that thirsts for thee eternally,
  Commands us, to His arms thy soul to chase;
He pours His light and grace,
    And courtesy,
    All, all on thee,
In spreading streams of Love!"

More would I love, if more were possible;
  Yet can I give no more than all my heart;
I give my all—my life, my soul, my will,
  Nor needs it proof that all is more than part.
I give Thee all, O Lover Terrible—
  Take all, fresh life for ever to impart;
So old, so new, Thou art;
    Yea, I have found Thee,
    Soft light around Thee,
And whiter than the Dove.

Gazing on Thee, Thou Bright and Morning Star,
  I am led far, I know not where I be;
My heart is melted like a waxen bar,
  That moulded in Christ's likeness it may be;
O Christ, Thy barters keen and wondrous are!
  I am stript naked, to be drest in Thee:
  My heart transformed in me,
    My mind lies dumb,
    To see Thee come,
In sweetness and in Love.

So linked with that sweetness is my mind,
  It leans and strains, its Lover to embrace:
And all in Him, and naught in self to find,

It learns, by gazing ever on His face.
Riches, and powers, and memories strong to bind
It casts away, as burdens in the race;
It hath no resting place,
No will, no care;
It mounts the stair,
Towards which its being strove.

. . .

I once could speak, but now my lips are dumb;
My eyes are blind, although I once could see:
In this abyss my soul is stark and numb,
Silent, I speak; cling, yet am held by Thee:
Falling, I rise; I go, and yet I come;
Pursue, and am pursued; I am bound yet free;
O Love that whelmeth me!
Maddened I cry:
"Why must I die,
Thy fiery strength to prove?"

. . .

Love, Love, of naught but Love my tongue can sing,
Thy wounded Hand hath pierced my heart so deep:
Love, Love, with Thee made one, to Thee I cling,
Upon Thy breast, my Jesu, let me sleep;
Love, Love, with Love my heart is perishing;
Love, like an Eagle snatching me Thy sleep,
For Thee I swoon, I weep,
Love, let me be,
By courtesy,
Thine own in death, O Love!

. . .

Love, Love, O Love, the world's wild voices cry,
Love, Love, O Love, the clamorous echoes spread;

Love, Love, O Love, so deep Thy treasures lie,
We hunger more, the more we taste Thy bread:
Love, Love, O Love, Thou Circling Mystery,
Who enters Thee at Love's deep heart is fed;
Thou'rt Loom, and Cloth, and Thread:
O sweet to be
Clad all in Thee
And ceaseless chant of Love.

Love, Love, O Love, Thy touch so quickens me,
Love, Love, O Love, I am no longer I:
Love, Love, O Love, Thyself so utterly
Thou giv'st me, Jesu, that I can but die.
O Love, O Love, I am possessed of Thee,
Love, Love, my Love, O take me in a sigh!
Love, glad and spent I lie.
O Love, my Bliss!
O Lover's Kiss!
O quench my soul in Love!

ST. JOHN OF THE CROSS

Union!

Without support, yet well supported,
Though in pitch-darkness, with no ray,
Entirely I am burned away.

My spirit is so freed from every
Created thing, that through the skies,
Above herself, she's lifted, flies,
And as in a most fragrant reverie,
Only on God her weight applies.

The thing which most my faith esteems
For this one fact well reported—
Because my soul above me streams
Without support, yet well-supported.

What though I languish in the shades
As through my mortal life I go,
Not over-heavy is my woe,
Since if no glow my gloom invades,
With a celestial life I glow.
The love of such a life, I say,
The more benightedly it darkens,
Turns more to that to which it hearkens,
Though in pitch-darkness, with no ray.

Since I knew Love, I have been taught
He can perform most wondrous labors.
Though good and bad in me are neighbors,
He turns their differences to naught,
Then both into Himself, so sweetly,
And with a flame so fine and fragrant
Which now I feel in me completely
Reduce my being, till no vagrant
Vestige of my own self can stay.
And wholly I am burned away.

KABIR

Lost in the Sky of Love

The shadows of evening fall thick
and deep, and the darkness of love
envelops the body and the mind.

Open the window to the west, and be
lost in the sky of love;
Drink the sweet honey that steeps the
petals of the lotus of the heart.
Receive the waves in your body: what
splendor is in the region of the
sea!
Hark! the sounds of conches and bells
are rising.
Kabir says: "O brother, behold! the
Lord is in this vessel of my body."

Path of the Infinite

Open your eyes of love, and see Him
who pervades this world! consider
it well, and know that this is your
own country.
When you meet the true Guru, He
will awaken your heart;
He will tell you the secret of love and
detachment, and then you will
know indeed that He transcends
this universe.
This world is the City of Truth, its
maze of paths enchants the heart:
We can reach the goal without crossing
the road, such is the sport unending.
Where the ring of manifold joys ever
dances about Him, there is the
sport of Eternal Bliss.

When we know this, then all our
 receiving and renouncing is over;
Thenceforth the heat of having shall
 never scorch us more.
He is the Ultimate Rest unbounded:
He has spread His form of love
 throughout all the world.
From that Ray which is Truth, streams
 of new forms are perpetually
 springing: and He pervades those
 forms.
All the gardens and groves and bowers
 are abounding with blossom; and
 the air breaks forth into ripples
 of joy.
There the swan plays a wonderful
 game,
There the Unstruck Music eddies
 around the Infinite One;
There, in the midst, the Throne of the
 Unheld is shining, whereon the
 great Being sits—
Millions of suns are shamed by the
 radiance of a single hair of His body.
On the harp of the road what true
 melodies are being sounded! and
 its notes pierce the heart:
There the Eternal Fountain is playing
 its endless life-streams of birth and
 death.
They call Him Emptiness Who is the
 Truth of truths, in Whom all
 truths are stored!

There within Him creation goes forward, which is beyond all philosophy; for philosophy cannot attain to Him;
There is an endless world, O my Brother! and there is the Nameless Being, of whom naught can be said.
Only he knows it who has reached that region: it is other than all that is heard and said.
No form, no body, no length, no breadth is seen there: how can I tell you that which it is?
He comes to the Path of the Infinite on whom the grace of the Lord descends: he is freed from births and deaths who attains to Him.
Kabir says: "It cannot be told by the words of the mouth, it cannot be written on paper:
It is like a dumb person who tastes a sweet thing—how shall it be explained?"

This Body, His Lyre

O friend! this body is His lyre;
He tightens its strings, and draws from it the melody of Brahma.
If the strings snap and the keys slacken, then to dust must this instrument of dust return:
Kabir says, "None but Brahma can evoke its melodies."

Love and Wisdom Are One

The light of the sun, the moon, and
the stars shine bright:
The melody of love swells forth, and
the rhythm of love's detachment
beats the time.
Day and night, the chorus of music
fills the heavens; and Kabir
says,
"My Beloved One gleams like the
lightning flash in the sky."

Do you know how the moments perform their adoration?
Waving its row of lamps, the universe
sings in worship day and night,
There are the hidden banner and the
secret canopy:
There the sound of the unseen bells is
heard.
Kabir says: "There adoration never
ceases; there the Lord of the
Universe sitteth on His throne.

The whole world does its works and
commits its errors: but few are
the lovers who know the Beloved.

. . .

Behold what wonderful rest is in the
Supreme Spirit! and he enjoys it,
who makes himself meet for it.

Held by the cords of love, the swing of
the Ocean of Joy sways to and fro;
and a mighty sound breaks forth
in song.
See what a lotus blooms there without
water! and Kabir says,
"My heart's bee drinks its nectar."

What a wonderful lotus it is, that
blooms at the heart of the spinning
wheel of the universe! Only a few
pure souls know of its true delight.
Music is all around it, and there the
heart partakes of the joy of the
Infinite Sea.
Kabir says: "Dive thou into the
Ocean of sweetness: thus let all
errors of life and of death flee
away."

Behold how the thirst of the five
senses is quenched there! and the
three forms of misery are no more!
Kabir says: "It is the sport of the
Unattainable One: look within,
and behold how the moonbeams
of that Hidden One shine in you."

There falls the rhythmic beat of life
and death:
Rapture wells forth, and all space is
radiant with light.

There the Unstruck Music is sounded;
it is the music of the love of the
three worlds.
There millions of lamps of sun and of
moon are burning;
There the drum beats, and the lover
swings in play.
There love-songs resound, and light
rains in showers; and the worshipper is entranced in the taste
of the heavenly nectar.

Look upon life and death; there is no
separation between them,
The right hand and the left hand are
one and the same.
Kabir says: "There the wise man is
speechless;
For this truth may
never be found in Vedas or in
books."

I have had my Seat on the Self-poised One,
I have drunk of the Cup of the Ineffable,
I have found the Key of the Mystery,
I have reached the Root of Union.
Travelling by no track, I have come
to the Sorrowless Land: very
easily has the mercy of the great
Lord come upon me.
They have sung of Him as infinite and
unattainable: but I in my medita-
tions have seen Him without sight.

That is indeed the sorrowless land, and
none know the path that leads
there:
Only he who is on that path has surely
transcended all sorrow.
Wonderful is that land of rest, to which
no merit can win;
It is the wise who has seen it, it is
the wise who has sung of it.
This is the Ultimate Word: but can
any express its marvelous savor?
He who has savored it once, he
knows what joy it can give.
Kabir says: "Knowing it, the ignorant
man becomes wise, and the
wise man becomes speechless and
silent,
The worshipper is utterly inebriated,
His wisdom and his detachment are
made perfect;
He drinks from the cup of the in-
breathings and the outbreathings
of love."

There the whole sky is filled with
sound, and there that music is
made without fingers and without
strings;
There the game of pleasure and pain
does not cease.
Kabir says: "If you merge your life
in the Ocean of Life, you will
find your life in the Supreme
Land of Bliss."

What a frenzy of ecstasy there is in
every hour! and the worshipper
is pressing out and drinking the
essence of the hours: he lives in
the life of Brahma.
I speak truth, for I have accepted
truth in life; I am now attached
to truth, I have swept all tinsel
away.
Kabir says: "Thus is the worshipper
set free from fear; thus have all
errors of life and of death left him."

There the sky is filled with music:
There it rains nectar:
There the harp-strings jingle,
there the drums beat.
What a secret splendor is there, in
the mansion of the sky!
There no mention is made of the rising
and the setting of the sun;
In the ocean of manifestation, which
is the light of love, day and night
are felt to be one.
Joy for ever, no sorrow, no struggle!
There have I seen joy filled to the
brim, perfection of joy;
No place for error is there.
Kabir says: "There have I witnessed
the sport of One Bliss!"

I have known in my body the sport
of the universe: I have escaped
from the error of this world.

The inward and the outward are
become as one sky, the Infinite
and the finite are united: I am
drunken with the sight of this
All!
This light of Thine fills the universe:
the lamp of love that burns
on the salver of knowledge.
Kabir says: "There error cannot
enter and the conflict of life and
death is felt no more."

KRISHNAMURTI

My Beloved and I Are One

As the aspen leaf is aquiver
With the breeze,
So my heart dances with Thy love.
As two mountain streams meet
With a roar,
Joyous in their exultation,
So have I met Thee, O my Beloved.

As the mountain top is aglow
At the going down of the sun,
Giving to the valley an immense desire,
So hast Thou given glory to my being.
As the valley is still at eventide,
So hast Thou calmed my soul.

My heart is filled
With the love of a thousand years.
Mine eyes
Behold Thy vision.

As the stars make the night beauteous,
So hast Thou given beauty to my soul.
As serene as the graven image
Have I become.

As the seed grows into a wondrous tree,
The abode of many joyous birds,
Giving soft shadows
To the weary traveller,
So has my soul grown
In search of Thee.

As a great river joins the sea,
So to Thee have I come,
Rich with my long journey
Full with the experience of an age.
O Beloved,
As the dewdrop
Mingles with the honey
Of the flower,
So Thou and I have become one.
O my Beloved,
Now there is no separation,
No loneliness,
No sorrow, no struggle.
Where'er I go,
I bring the glory of Thy presence.
For, O Beloved
Thou and I are one.

Thou Art There

Wherever I look, Thou art there.
I am full of Thy glory.
I am burning with Thy happiness.
I weep for all men
That do not behold Thee.
In what manner
Shall I show them
Thy glory?

I sat a-dreaming in a room of great silence,
The early morning was still and breathless,
The great blue mountains stood against the dark skies, cold and clear,
Round the dark log house
The black and yellow birds were welcoming the sun.

I sat on the floor, with legs crossed, meditating,
Forgetting the blue sunlit mountains,
The birds,
The immense silence,
And the golden sun.

I lost the feel of my body,
My limbs were motionless,
Relaxed and at peace,
A great joy of unfathomable depth filled my heart.
Eager and keen was my mind, concentrated.
Lost the transient world,
I was full of strength.

As the Eastern breeze,
That suddenly springs into being,

And calms the weary world,
There in front of me
Seated, cross-legged, as the world knows Him,
In His yellow robes, simple and magnificent,
Was the Teacher of Teachers.

Looking at me,
Motionless, the Mighty Being sat.
I looked and bowed my head,
My body bent forward of itself.

That one look
Showed the progress of the world,
Showed the immense distance between the world
And the greatest of its Teachers.

How little it understood,
And how much He gave.
How joyously He soared,
Escaping from birth and death,
From its tyranny and entangling wheel.

Enlightenment attained,
He gave to the world, as the flower gives
Its scent,
The Truth.

As I looked
At the sacred feet that once trod the happy
Dust of India,
My heart poured forth its devotion,
Limitless and unfathomable,
Without restraint and without effort.

I lost myself in that happiness.
My mind so easily and strangely
Understood the Truth
He longed for and attained.
I lost myself in that happiness.
My soul grasped the infinite simplicity
Of Truth.
I lost myself in that happiness.

Thou art the Truth,
Thou art the Law,
Thou art the Refuge,
Thou art the Guide,
The Companion and the Beloved.
Thou hast ravished my heart,
Thou hast conquered my soul,
In Thee have I found my comfort,
In Thee is my Truth established.

Where Thou hast trodden
Do I follow.
Where Thou hast suffered and conquered,
Do I gather strength.
Where Thou hast renounced,
Do I grow,
Dispassionate, detached.

Like the stars
Have I become.
Happy is he that knoweth Thee
Eternally.

Like the sea, unfathomable
Is my love.
The Truth have I attained,
And calm grows my spirit.

But yesterday
I longed to withdraw
From the aching world
Into some secluded mountain spot,
Untrammeled,
Free,
Away from all things,
In search of Thee.
And now Thou hast appeared
Unto me.

I carry Thee in my heart.
Look where I may, Thou art there,
Calm, happy,
Filling my world—
The embodiment of Truth.

My heart is strong,
My mind is concentrated,
I am full of Thee.
As the Eastern breeze
That suddenly springs into being,
And calms the weary world,
So have I realized.

I am the Truth,
I am the Law,
I am the Refuge,
I am the Guide,
The Companion and the Beloved.

LALLESWARI

Thee, in All I See

Loose the sugar load upon my back:
Sling and knot do my poor shoulder gall:
Crooked hath my day's work gone, alack.
How can I bear with it, ere I fall?

Seeking my teacher, I heard Him tell
Truths that like a blister hurt my heart—
Pain of lost illusion loved so well.
How can I bear with it, ere we part?

Flocks of my consciousness all are lost,
Gone from the shepherd beyond recall,
Ere the mountain of Release be crossed;
How can I bear with it ere I fall?

Searching and seeking from my inner soul
Came I to the moon of knowledge bright:
Searching and seeking, I learnt the whole
Truth that like shall with like unite.

O Naran, the All is only Thou.
Only Thee, Naran, in all I see.
O Naran, the sports Thou showest now
Are but clear illusions unto me.

Learning myself to be Self Supreme,
I have learnt, Naran, why Thou dost part:
I have solved the Riddle of the Dream,
Where we twain do as one Self consort.

MECHTHILD OF MAGDEBURG

Thy Love and Mine Is One

"Come love! Sing on me and let Me hear
How thou canst sing this song!"

"Alas! beloved! My throat is parched
From my maidenly innocence . . .

"Yet the sweetness of thy gentleness
Brings back music to my voice
So that I now can sing this song—
  'Lord! Thy blood and mine is one unstained;
  Thy love and mine is one and undivided;
  Thy robe and mine is one, unspotted,
  Thy lips and mine are one, unkissed . . .'
Such are the words of the song of love:
May the sweet music of the heart ever remain in it,
For no earthly pen could ever describe it!"

God Answers the Soul

That I love thee continuously is My Nature
For I Myself am Love;
That I love thee fervently is My Desire
For I long to be greatly loved.
That I love thee long comes from My Eternity
For I am everlasting and without end.

METTIKA

Buddha's Will Is Done

Though I be suffering and weak, and all
My youthful spring be gone, yet have I come,
Leaning upon my staff, and climb aloft
The mountain peak.
My cloak thrown off,
My little bowl o'erturned: so sit I here
Upon the rock. And o'er my spirit sweeps
The breath of Liberty! I win, I win
The Triple Lore! The Buddha's will is done!

PATACARA

My Heart Is Free

With ploughshares ploughing up the fields, with seed
Sown in the breast of earth, men with their crops,
Enjoy their gains and nourish wife and child.
Why cannot I, whose life is pure, who seek
To do the Master's will, no sluggard am
Nor puffed up, win to Nibbana's bliss?

One day, bathing my feet, I sit and watch
The water as it trickles down the slope.
Thereby I set my heart in steadfastness,
As one doth train a horse of noble breed.
Then going to my call, I take my lamp,
And seated on my couch I watch the flame.

Grasping the pin, I pull the wick right down
Into the oil. . . .
Lo! the Nibbana of the little lamp!
Emancipation dawns! My heart is free!

RABI'A

With My Beloved Alone

With my Beloved I alone have been,
When secrets tenderer than evening airs
Passed, and the Vision blest
Was granted to my prayers,
That crowned me, else obscure, with endless fame;
The while amazed between
His Beauty and His Majesty
I stood in silent ecstasy
Revealing that which o'er my spirit went and came.
Lo, in His face commingled
Is every charm and grace;
The whole of Beauty singled
Into a perfect face
Beholding Him would cry,
"There is no God but He, and He is the most High."

ANGELUS SILESIUS

The Known Must Be the Knower

In God nought e'er is known.
Forever one is He.
What we in Him e'er know
Ourselves must grow and be.

RUMI

Unknowing

Lo, for I to myself am unknown, now in God's name what must I
do?
I adore not the Cross or the Crescent, I am not a Giaour or a Jew.
East nor West, land nor sea is my home; I have kin nor with angel
nor gnome;
I am wrought not of fire nor of foam, I am shaped not of dust nor of
dew.
I was born not in China afar, not in Saqsin and not in Bulghar;
Not in India, where five rivers are, nor Iraq nor Khorasan I grew.
Not in this world nor that world I dwell, not in Paradise, neither in
Hell;
Not from Eden and Rizwan* I fell, not from Adam my lineage I
drew.
In a place beyond uttermost place, in a tract without shadow of trace,
Soul and body transcending, I live in the Soul of my Loved One
anew!

ST. TERESA OF AVILA

My Beloved One Is Mine

I gave myself to Love Divine,
And lo! my lot so changed is
That my Beloved One is mine
And I at last am surely His.

When that sweet Huntsman from above
First wounded me and left me prone,

* Rizwan, the Angel who keeps the keys of Paradise.

Into the very arms of Love
My stricken soul forthwith was thrown.
Since then my life's no more my own
And all my lot so changed is
That my Beloved One is mine
And I at last am surely His.

The dart wherewith He wounded me
Was all embarbed round with love,
And thus my spirit came to be
One with its Maker, God above.
No love but this I need to prove:
My life to God surrender'd is
And my Beloved One is mine
And I at last am surely His.

TAYUMANAVAR

Fulfillment

Marvelous indeed was the expedient,
by which you took me to be your own
and said "Be still," so that I sank within
and became That, that floodtide of Bliss.

SWAMI VIVEKANANDA

Hymn of Samadhi

Lo! The sun is not, nor the comely moon,
All light extinct; in the great void of space
Floats shadow-like the image-universe.

In the void of mind involute, there floats
The fleeting universe, rises and floats,
Sinks again, ceaseless, in the current "I."

Slowly, slowly, the shadow-multitude
Entered the primal womb, and flowed ceaseless,
The only current, the "I am," "I am."

Lo! 'Tis stopped, ev'n that current flows no more,
Void merged into void—beyond speech and mind!
Whose heart understands, he verily does.

The Song of the Free

The wounded snake its hood unfurls,
The flame stirred up doth blaze,
The desert air resounds the calls
Of heart-struck lion's rage:

The cloud puts forth its deluge strength
When lightning cleaves its breast,
When the soul is stirred to its inmost depth
Great ones unfold their best!

Let eyes grow dim and heart grow faint
And friendship fail and love betray,
Let Fate its hundred horrors send
And clotted darkness block the way—

All nature wears one angry frown
To crush you out—still know, my soul,
You are Divine. March on and on,
Nor right nor left, but to the goal!

Nor angel I, nor man nor brute,
Nor body, mind, nor he nor she;
The books do stop in wonder mute
To tell my nature—I am He!

Before the sun, the moon, the earth,
Before the stars or comets free,
Before e'en Time has had its birth
I was, I am and I will be!

The beauteous earth, the glorious sun,
The calm sweet moon, the spangled sky,
Causation's laws do make them run,
They live in bonds, in bonds they die—

And mind its mantle, dreamy net,
Casts o'er them all and holds them fast.
In warp and woof of thought are set
Earth, hells and heavens, or worst or best.

Know these are but the outer crust—
All space and time, all effect, cause,
I am beyond all sense, all thought,
The Witness of the Universe!

Not two nor many, 'tis but One.
And thus in me all ones I have,
I cannot hate, I cannot shun
Myself from me—I can but love!

From dream awake, from bonds be free!
Be not afraid. This mystery,
My shadow, cannot frighten me!
Know once for all that I am He!

Glossary

GLOSSARY OF SANSKRIT WORDS USED IN THIS ANTHOLOGY

Adharma Unrighteousness; the absence of virtue.
Ahamkar Ego-sense.
Bhakti Devotion (to God).
Buddhi Discriminating faculty; intellect.
Chitta Mind-stuff.
Deva A god.
Dharma Righteous living; the way of life a man's nature imposes on him.
Guru Spiritual teacher; illumined soul.
Japam The practice of chanting a name of God.
Jiva The individual soul.
Kali Divine Mother of the Universe.
Karma Action; work; the result of one's past deeds.
Mâyâ Apparent reality; phenomenal world.
Mukti Final liberation from worldly bondage.
Om (Aum) Universal symbol for Brahman in His personal as well as impersonal aspect: the Logos.
Nibbana Nirvana; God-realization; supreme God-union.
Prema Ecstatic love (of God).
Sakti Female energy; God the Mother.
Samadhi God-realization; highest state of mystical union.
Samsâr(a) The ceaseless cycle of birth, death and rebirth.
Sannyas The monastic life.
Tapasya An act of austerity.
Tapa Spiritual discipline; austerity.
Tyâga Renunciation; detachment.
Yaksha A demi-god.

Biographical Notes

BIOGRAPHICAL NOTES

ANSARI (1005–1088). Sufi mystic and poet. Author of *Minajat*, a collection of prayers in prose and short poems, and *Manazil al-Sa'irin*, which sketches the Sufi path to God.

'ATTAR, FARID ED DIN (ca. 1130–1230). Persian mystic and author of a reputed 45,000 couplets.

BABA KUHI (*of Shiraz*) (died A.D. 1050). Persian poet.

BABA TAHIR (ca. 10th century). A wandering mystic known as "the distracted lover of God."

DA TODI, JACOPONE (1228–1306). The most profound 13th-century Italian mystical poet. A lawyer until age 40, when he became a missionary hermit. Ten years later, he entered the Franciscan family as a lay brother.

DHU'L-NUN AL-MIRSI (786–857). Sufi mystic. ("The food of my soul is the remembrance of God.")

FAKHIR AL-DIN MAS'UDI (Before the 12th century). Sufi mystic.

IBN-GABIROL, SOLOMON (1021–1069?). Jewish poet and philosopher, born in the South of Spain.

'IRAQI, FAKHRU'DDIN (1211–1289). One of the greatest Persian poets of the 13th century.

IQBAL, MUHAMMAD (1897–1938). Sufi poet-writer. Studied Western philosophy, receiving degrees from Cambridge and Munich.

JAMI, NUR-ADDIN 'ABN-ALRAHMAN (1414–1492). Erudite, self-taught Persian mystic-poet.

JENTI (JENTA). Buddhist nun.

JOHN, ST., OF THE CROSS (1542–1591). The most famous Christian mystic, born in Spain. His mystical writings, both poetry and prose, reveal great psychological insight. A Carmelite monk, he was St. Teresa's spiritual confessor.

KABIR (1440–1518). A joyous God-lover and mystical poet, he worked as a weaver, while worshipping God. He was a disciple of the celebrated Hindu ascetic Ramananda.

KRISHNAMURTI, JIDDI (1895–). Born in South India, educated in England. Widely known and respected as a religious-philosophical thinker, writer, and speaker.

LAO-TZU (604–570 B.C.). "Golden Age" Chinese mystic and founder of Taoism, he taught "the way of life."

LALLESWARI (LAL DIDDI) of Kashmir. Woman mystic-poet of the 14th century. Considered the best exponent of Savism. (Savism accepts the monistic philosophy of the Vedanta.)

LEON, LUIS DE. Born ca. 1527 at Belmonte de Cuenca, Spain, allegedly of Jewish descent. Entered the Augustinian Order at fifteen. Considered the equal of St. John of the Cross as a lyric poet. (Most of his works are not in English translation.)

MANIKKAVACHAGAR (9th century). Poet, saint. His great work, *Tiruvachagam* (book of psalms) has been studied by Eastern and Western scholars.

SISTER MARCELA DE CARPIO DE SAN FELIX (16th century). Christian nun.

MECHTHILD OF MAGDEBURG (1207–1294). Great German woman mystic of the Middle Ages, of Christ. Entered House of Beguines at twenty-six. (Beguine Houses were religious sisterhoods, dedicated to charity, sick-nursing, and devotion to God.)

METTIKA. Buddhist nun. Born of eminent Brahmin parents at Rajagaha.

MIRA BAI (16th century). Famous throughout India as a lover of Krishna (God in His personal aspect), for whom she continuously composed her mystical love song-poems. Renouncing her princess title, Mira Bai devoted herself entirely to God alone, singing His glories and making holy pilgrimages.

MUKERJI, DHAN GOPAL (1890–1936). Indian-American novelist-writer. Born in Calcutta of a Brahmin family. Wrote children's books, as well as cultural (Indian) and religious poetry, prose, and fiction.

NANAK (Born 1469 in Punjab, India). Founded Sikh religion. Author of *Japji*, 38 psalms of praises in remembrance of the Lord.

NI'MAT-ALLAH (1330–1431). Renowned Persian poet and saint.

PATACARA. Mystic nun of the Bhikkhunis Order, devotees of Buddha.

QUARLES, FRANCIS (1592–1644). Christian mystic and scholar.

RABI'A (717–801). Famous Sufi woman mystic, born in Islam. Revered as a supreme lover of God, her teachings were sought by many respected men and women of her time. ("My love for God has so possessed me that no place remains for loving or hating anyone save Him.")

REVIUS, JACOB (Born in The Netherlands). He taught as a Calvinist minister. In his poetry, form and vision skilfully combine.

ROLLE, RICHARD. Born ca. 1290 in Yorkshire, England. Devout lover of Christ, he lived a celibate life of contemplation and wrote religious love lyrics. Influenced by the Franciscans.

RUMI, JALAL-ED DIN (1207–1273). Considered the greatest mystical poet of Persia. He composed over 2,000 mystical odes.

SANA'I (ca. 1046–1141). Persian mystic. Born at Ghazna.

SANKARA DEVI (1449– ?). Born in India. A lover of God as well as a scholar.

SILESIUS, ANGELUS (1624– ?). Born Johannes Scheffler at Silesia. A Protestant, his public conversion to the Catholic Church occurred at twenty-nine. He was greatly influenced by the Christian mystic, Jacob Boehme.

SISUPACALA. Buddhist nun.

SUJATA. Buddhist nun.

SUNDARI-NANDA. A sister in the Buddha era. The name literally means "beautiful delight."

TAYUMANAVAR. A lyrical and mystical poet and saint whose life expressed an harmonization of knowledge and devotion to God.

TERESA, ST., OF AVILA (1515–1582). Famous for her visions and spiritual ecstasies born of her single-minded devotion to God. She entered the Augustinian convent of St. Mary of Grace at twenty-one.

TUKARAM (1598–1649). Poet and saint of Maharashtra. Member of the Maratha sect of India.

VIVEKANANDA, SWAMI (1863–1902). Intimate disciple of Sri Ramakrishna, modern saint of India, he introduced the eternal Vedanta to the West in 1893, when he spoke at the World Parliament of Religions in Chicago. A dynamic figure, his holiness, intense love of God, and scholarship attracted interested students, and at their request he held classes abroad and in America. His published works, which include letters, poetry, lectures, and "inspired talks," are an excellent presentation of mysticism. His life exemplified the harmony of the four paths of yoga (union with God): *viz.*, love, wisdom, inner contemplation, and selfless activity.

Further Reading

RECOMMENDATIONS FOR FURTHER READING

On Mysticism in General:

BLAKNEY, RAYMOND B. *Meister Eckhart.* A Modern Translation. New York, 1941.

CHENEY, SHELDON. *Men Who Have Walked with God.* New York, 1956.

DASGUPTA, S. N. *Hindu Mysticism.* New York, 1959.

FORMAN, HENRY J. AND GAMMON, R. *Truth Is One.* New York.

HAPPOLD, F. C. *Mysticism—A Study and Anthology.* New York, 1963.

HUXLEY, ALDOUS. *Perennial Philosophy.* New York, 1962.

ISHERWOOD, CHRISTOPHER. *Ramakrishna and His Disciples.* New York, 1965.

MARQUETTE, JACQUES. *Comparative Mysticism.* New York, 1949.

OTTO, RUDOLPH. *Mysticism East and West.* New York, 1957.

PEERS, E. ALLISON. *Studies of the Spanish Mystics.* London, 1927.

REINHOLD, HANS A. *The Soul Afire.* New York, 1960.

SCHOLEM, GERSHOM G. *Major Trends in Jewish Mysticism.* New York, 1954.

SMITH, MARGARET. *The Sufi Path of Love—An Anthology of Sufism.* London, 1954.

SPENCER, SIDNEY. *Mysticism in World Religions.* New York, 1963.

STACE, WALTER T. *Teachings of the Mystics.* New York, 1960.

UNDERHILL, EVELYN. *Essentials of Mysticism.* New York, 1960.

———. *Mysticism.* New York, 1962.

———. *Mystics of the Church.* New York, 1964.

VIVEKANANDA, SWAMI. *Complete Works.* (8 Vols.) Calcutta, 1962.

On Mysticism and Poetry:

GUPTA, NOLINI KANTA. *Poets and Mystics.* Madras, 1951.

HUSAIN, ITRAT. *Mystical Element in the Metaphysical Poets of the Seventeenth Century.* London, 1948.

NICHOLSON, R. A., trans. *Eastern Poetry and Prose.* New York, 1922.

On Mystical Poetry and Poets:

ARBERRY, ARTHUR J. *'Iraqi: The Song of Lovers.* Calcutta, 1939.

BEHARI, BANKEY. *Bhakta Mira.* Bombay, 1961.

CAMPBELL, ROY, trans. *St. John of the Cross Poems.* New York, 1957.

MENZIES, LUCY, trans. *The Revelations of Mechthild of Magdeburg.* London, 1953.

NICHOLSON, R.A., trans. *Rumi—Poet and Mystic.* London, 1950.

PEERS, E. ALLISON. *Complete Works of St. Teresa.* London, 1950.

SILESIUS, ANGELUS. *The Cherubic Wanderer.* New York, 1953.

SMITH, MARGARET. *Rabi'a the Mystic.* London, 1928.

TAGORE, RABINDRANATH, trans. *One Hundred Poems of Kabir.* London, 1961.

Indexes

INDEX OF TITLES AND FIRST LINES

INDEX OF AUTHORS AND POEMS